Anonymous

Fundamental Problems

the method of philosophy as a systematic arrangement of knowledge

Anonymous

Fundamental Problems
the method of philosophy as a systematic arrangement of knowledge

ISBN/EAN: 9783337080013

Printed in Europe, USA, Canada, Australia, Japan

Cover: Foto ©Thomas Meinert / pixelio.de

More available books at **www.hansebooks.com**

FUNDAMENTAL PROBLEMS.

THE

METHOD OF PHILOSOPHY

AS A

SYSTEMATIC ARRANGEMENT OF KNOWLEDGE

BY

DR. PAUL CARUS.

No Agnosticism but Positive Science,
No Mysticism but Clear Thought,
Neither Supernaturalism nor Materialism,
But a Unitary Conception of the World,
No Dogma but Religion,
No Creed but Faith.

CHICAGO:
THE OPEN COURT PUBLISHING COMPANY
1889.

GEMS FROM MARCUS AURELIUS ANTONINUS.

Εἴ τίς με ἐλέγξαι, καὶ παραστῆσαί μοι ὅτι οὐκ ὀρθῶς ὑπολαμβάνω ἢ πράσσω, δύναται, χαίρων μεταθήσομαι· ζητῶ γὰρ τὴν ἀλήθειαν, ὑφ' ἧς οὐδεὶς πώποτε ἐβλάβη. Βλάπτεται δὲ ὁ ἐπιμένων ἐπὶ τῆς ἑαυτοῦ ἀπάτης καὶ ἀγνοίας.—VI. 21.

[If any man is able to convince me and show me that I do not think or act right, I will gladly change. For I seek the truth by which no man was ever injured. But he is injured who abides in his error and ignorance.]

Ἤτοι κόσμος διατεταγμένος, ἢ κυκεών, συμπεφορημένος μὲν ἀλλὰ κόσμος. Ἢ ἐν σοὶ μέν τις κόσμος ὑφίστασθαι δύναται, ἐν δὲ τῷ παντὶ ἀκοσμία;—IV. 27.

[Either it is a cosmos or a chaos, driven together—but still a cosmos. But can a cosmos subsist in thee and disorder in the All ?]

Πάντα ἀλλήλοις ἐπιπλέκεται καὶ ἡ σύνδεσις ἱερά, καὶ σχεδόν τι οὐδὲν ἀλλότριον ἄλλο ἄλλῳ. Συγκατατέτακται γάρ, καὶ συγκοσμεῖ τὸν αὐτὸν κόσμον. Κόσμος τε γὰρ εἷς ἐξ ἁπάντων, καὶ θεὸς εἷς διὰ πάντων, καὶ οὐσία μία, καὶ νόμος εἷς, λόγος κοινὸς πάντων τῶν νοερῶν ζῴων, καὶ ἀλήθεια μία ·—VII. 9.

[All things are connected with one another and the bond is holy. There is hardly anything foreign to any other thing. For things have been coördinated and they combine to form one and the same cosmos. For there is one cosmos made up of all things and one God who pervades all things and one substance, one law, one common reason in all intelligent animals and one truth.]

Ἥ τε γὰρ οὐσία οἷον ποταμὸς ἐν διηνεκεῖ ῥύσει· καὶ αἱ ἐνέργειαι ἐν συνεχέσι μεταβολαῖς, καὶ τὰ αἴτια ἐν μυρίαις τροπαῖς· καὶ σχεδὸν οὐδὲν ἑστῶς καὶ τὸ πάρεγγυς·—V. 23.

[Substance is like a river in a continual flow ; the energies undergo constant changes and cause work in infinite varieties. There is hardly anything that stands still or remains the same.]

Διέλε καὶ μέρισον τὸ ὑποκείμενον εἰς τὸ αἰτιῶδες καὶ ὑλικόν.–VII. 29.

[Separate and divide the object in the formal and the material.]

Ἐξ αἰτιώδους καὶ ὑλικοῦ συνέστηκα· οὐδέτερον δὲ τούτων εἰς τὸ μὴ ὂν φθαρήσεται· ὥσπερ οὐδὲ ἐκ τοῦ μὴ ὄντος ὑπέστη.–V. 13.

[I consist of the formal and of the material. Neither will be lost in nothing, nor did either come from nothing.]

Ἔνδον βλέπε. Ἔνδον ἡ πηγὴ τοῦ ἀγαθοῦ, καὶ ἀεὶ ἀναβλύειν δυναμένη, ἐὰν ἀεὶ σκάπτης.–VII. 59.

[Look within! Within is the fountain of good and it will ever well up if thou wilt ever dig.]

Λῃστὴς προαιρέσεως οὐ γίνεται· τὸ τοῦ Ἐπικτήτου.–XI. 36.

[No one can rob us of our free will, says Epictetus.]

Ἕκαστον πρός τι γέγονεν· Σὺ οὖν πρὸς τί; τὸ ἥδεσθαι; ἴδε, εἰ ἀνέχεται ἡ ἔννοια.–VIII. 19.

[Everything exists for some end. For what end, then, art thou? To enjoy pleasure? See whether common sense allows this.]

Ἡδονῶν καὶ πόνων καθυπερτερεῖν ἔξεστιν.–VIII. 8.

[Thou canst master pleasure and pain.]

Οὔτε ἄρα χρήσιμον, οὔτε ἀγαθὸν ἡδονή.–VIII. 10.

[Pleasure is neither useful nor good.]

Πᾶν μοι συναρμόζει, ὃ σοὶ εὐάρμοστόν ἐστιν, ὦ κόσμε. Οὐδέν μοι πρόωρον, οὐδὲ ὄψιμον, τὸ σοὶ εὔκαιρον. Πᾶν μοι καρπός, ὃ φέρουσιν αἱ σαὶ ὧραι, ὦ φύσις· ἐκ σοῦ πάντα, ἐν σοὶ πάντα, εἰς σὲ πάντα.
–IV. 23.

[Everything harmonizes with me which is harmonious to thee, O Cosmos. Nothing for me is too early nor too late which is in due time for thee. Everything is first to me which thy seasons bring, O Nature. From thee are all things, in thee are all things, to thee all things return.]

PREFACE.

ALMOST all of the essays of this book first appeared as editorial articles in THE OPEN COURT, where they had the good fortune of being exposed to the criticism of thoughtful readers. The ideas presented could thus be tested, and the views of the author received an opportunity of being further elucidated, not in futile battles against men of straw, but in discussions with thinkers who had found difficulties in understanding the solutions proposed. I here publicly acknowledge my indebtedness to the gentlemen who have favored me with criticisms.

*   *   *

The author, while working out in his mind the Fundamental Problems, has endeavored to introduce as little as possible of his personality and his private sympathies with, or antipathies against, other solutions. The brain of the philosopher should be a mental alembic to clarify ideas, to analyze them, to extract their essence. His brain should work with the regularity of a machine. And among machines the philosophical mind must be compared to the so-called *precision machines*, the work of which is not measured by horse-power but by minute exactitude.

The article "Form and Formal Thought" discusses a subject which is of fundamental importance. A correct conception of form and the laws of form will clear away many mysteries; it will afford a satisfactory explanation of causality and shed a new light on all the other problems of philosophy.

The view here presented, in spite of all our differences with Kant, may be considered as the natural outcome of Kant's philosophy. But it would be wrong to represent it as Kantianism. It is rather the historical development of Kantianism broadened by later enquiries, matured by criticisms, and adapted to the needs of our time. It is a protest against the halfness of agnosticism and a rejection of the perverted ethics of shallow hedonism—of that view so popular now, which bases the rules of conduct upon man's desire for happiness.

The view here presented unites two qualities which may appear contradictory at first sight. It is *radical* and at the same time *conservative.* It is radical because it fearlessly presents the issues of philosophic thought in their stern rigidity without trying to conceal the consequences to which the argument leads. The old and long cherished errors are not passed over in silence, but are countenanced and critically explained. The view propounded is at the same time conservative because it preserves its historical connection with the work of our ancestors ; it does not hope for a progress by a rupture with, but through a development from, the past, and does not come to destroy but to fulfill.

* * *

The purpose of philosophy has often been misunderstood. It is not grand and beautiful air castles, not ontological systems of pure thought, not new original ideas of what the dreamland of the Absolute might be like, that is wanted in philosophy. Philosophy is not a profitless intellectual gymnastics, not a mere playing with words and subtle distinctions for the gratification of a few *beaux esprits* who delight in mental somersaults. Philosophy is the most practical and most important science, because its prob-

lems lie at the bottom of all the single sciences. It is the science
of science.

· Philosophy is more than that. It is the foundation of the
rules of our conduct. Those conceptions of the world which have
become the popular philosophy of the age—the so-called *Zeitgeist*
—will permeate the whole atmosphere of the time and will influence the actions of men for good and for evil. The fates of individuals, as well as of nations, their prosperity and their ruin, always depended, and in future times will depend, upon their fundamental conceptions of the world, in accordance with which men
naturally regulate their conduct in·life.

It may be objected that Religion and Ethics, not Philosophy,
are the regulating factors of morality. But are not Religion and
Ethics expressions of certain fundamental conceptions of the world;
are they not applied philosophy? As a matter of fact history
teaches that the self-same religion under the influence of dif-
erent philosophies has developed into practically different systems of morality. Mohammedanism in the golden days of the
Caliphate of Cordova was different from that of Bagdad, and still
more from Mohammedanism as it exists to-day in Constantinople.
And Christianity, the most powerful religion in the world, shows
as many different phases as it has been influenced by different
philosophies or *Zeitgeists*.

We know of no decline of any nation on earth unless it was
preceded by an intellectual and moral rottenness, which took the
shape of some negative creed or skepticism, teaching the maxim
that man lives for the pleasure of living, and that the purpose of
our life is merely to enjoy ourselves.

The fashionable free thought of to-day is so closely connected with negativism and hedonism that most people are accustomed to identify free thought with these its excrescences. In this book, however, is proposed a philosophy of most radical free thought, that is *no* negativism, *no* agnosticism, and *no* metaphysical mysticism, but a systematic arrangement of positive facts. On the ground of positive facts, it equally opposes hedonism as well as asceticism, propounding a humanitarian ethics which, if obeyed, will keep our nation healthy and must lead us not on the easy path of "least resistance," but on the thorny and steep road of progress onward and upward to ever higher and nobler states of existence.

Our fundamental conceptions of world and life, therefore, for practical purposes—for our individual welfare, for the destiny of our nation and for that of humanity—are of greatest importance. On the philosophy of our time depends the health of our religious, our scientific, our industrial, our mercantile, our political, and our social development.

THE AUTHOR.

TABLE OF CONTENTS.

SENSATION AND MEMORY.

THE primal condition of knowledge is sensation. All knowledge has its root in sensation, and without sensation there could be no knowledge.

Sensation is a process which, under certain circumstances, takes place in living matter when influenced by its surroundings. Take for instance a moner which you may keep on a watch crystal in a drop of water. Expose the moner to light and the light will excite its activity; touch it with a pin, dipped before in acetic acid, it will flee from the offensive object. Throw something in its way on which it can feed and it will seize it. It will be affected differently by different things, but similarly under similar conditions, and will react accordingly.

Sensation is a psychical phenomenon. When a moner is affected by and responds to irritations, it behaves in such a way as to leave no doubt that there is on a small scale and in a very simple condition the selfsame power at work which we feel active in our consciousness. Like ourselves, the moner is a sentient being, a creature that is endowed with feeling. 'Psychical,' accordingly, we call all phenomena of sensation from the simplest feeling of pleasure or pain, or indifferent perceptive impressions to the most complex states of conscious thought and purposive will.

Mr. G. J. Romanes considers as the characteristic

feature of psychic acts the faculty of choice.* This may be true. In making a special selection, in giving preference to one kind of food or another, a micro-organism will best show its psychical qualities; but the essential feature of psychic life, it appears, is sensation or the property of feeling which we must suppose to accompany certain movements of a creature and which is most plainly recognized in the way a creature makes a choice. A sieve certainly discriminates also between the coarser and finer particles which are thrown on its wires, but no one will call the selection made in this way a psychical act on the part of the sieve.

Of the existence of feeling, we have the most intimate and immediate knowledge, for we ourselves are feeling. Feeling is a fact; it is the most indubitable fact of all; and all knowledge rests on it. Psychology accepts this fact as the basic datum of its investigations and must attempt to reduce all more complicated phenomena of psychic life to simple feelings.

Every single feeling appears to us most simple, but this does not exclude that, in fact, it is a very complicated phenomenon.

The question as to the origin of feeling is an unsolved problem still, and we cannot so soon hope for a satisfactory solution. This much, however, can be safely stated, that we must expect the solution of this problem from biological investigations. Feeling does not come into the protoplasma of organisms from transcendent spheres. The conditions of feeling must exist in the inorganic matter of our world, and the appearance of the phenomena of sensation, will be found

---

* See Alfred Binet, "The Psychic Life of Micro-Organisms," p. 109. Open Court Publishing Co., Chicago, Ill.

to depend upon a special form in which the molecules
of protoplasma combine and disintegrate.

If the same irritation, in a moner, is repeated, the
animalcule will show a greater ability to respond to
the occasion. In other words, the moner possesses
memory. A previous sensation has predisposed it to
react more readily to the second and third irritation
and we must ask, How is that possible?

We can observe that the irritation affecting the
moner produces certain chemical changes in its substance, and also the motions of the animalcule are in
the same way accompanied by such changes in the
protoplasma. The process of life, even if the creature
is at rest, is an unceasing activity. Oxygen is constantly being absorbed and food assimilated while the
waste products are excreted in the form of carbonic
acid and in other decompositions. The rebuilding of
the life-substance by assimilation takes place in such
a way as to preserve the old arrangement of molecules. Even on the skin of the hand a scar remains
visible years after the wound is healed, because the
form and arrangement once produced is preserved: it
is transmitted from the old substance to the new
growth of cells developing therefrom. This preservation and transmittance of form is the physiological
condition of memory. If certain changes which take
place in living substance are accompanied by sensation, the preservation of certain physiological forms,
produced by such changes, will preserve the corresponding forms of sensation also. They are registered
in the protoplasma similarly as a speech is recorded
on the tin-foil of the phonograph. If the physiological
forms of sentient matter are called into activity by
some stimulus, it will reproduce in a weaker form the

corresponding sensation just as the phonograph will reproduce the speech.

Memory, therefore, is the psychological aspect of the preservation of physiological forms in sentient substance and is as such the conditioning factor in the development of knowledge from sensation.

The arrangement of the molecules becomes more and more adapted to the impression of their surroundings. Thus under the constant influence of special irritations, special senses are created. Given ether-waves of light and sensation, and in the long process of evolution an eye will be formed; given air-waves of sound and sensation, and in the long process of evolution an ear will be formed. Thus sensation, with the assistance of memory adapting itself to its conditions, produces the different sense-organs.

The different sense-organs possess their "specific energies," as Johannes Müller calls their inherited memory* of reacting in a special and always the same way upon irritation. Irritations of the eye produce in the optic nerve sensations of light, and irritations of the ear produce in the auditory nerve sensations of sound, even if there be neither light nor sound, but other causes, as, for instance, electric currents. The percepts of vision are felt as images which we project outside of ourselves to places where, by the experience of touch, we have become accustomed to expect their presence.

A new percept of a thing that has been perceived before, will, under ordinary conditions, be recognized as the same. The new percept producing in the sensory nerves the same form of motion as the old per-

---

* See OPEN COURT, Nos. 6 and 7: Ewald Hering, "Memory as a General Function of Organized Matter."

cept of the same thing, finds certain brain-structures predisposed to receive it. Being produced in structures shaped by all the former percepts, it at the same time re-awakens their memories. All living bodies have thus become* store-houses of innumerable memories, which are treasured up since organized life began on earth and are transmitted and added to from generation to generation.

The percepts of our senses, being specialized acts of feeling, are the elements of our psychic life. They are the facts (or if you so please the ultimate facts) given by reality; and it is from them that we derive all the knowledge we have. From them all our abstractions grow, our concepts, our formal thought, our ideas, and even our ideals. All the higher intellectual and spiritual life of man's consciousness, the schemes of the inventor, the fancies of the poet, and the theories of the philosopher, blossom forth from, and can be reduced to, the simple data of perception.

The simple phenomenon of sensation has in the long process of evolution grown highly complex. The nerves of animals being centralized in the brain, their feelings form a multifarious unity which is called consciousness. The unity of consciousness is not (as has been supposed in former centuries) the life-principle, nor is it the soul of the animal, and still less is it a substance existing independent of the body of that creature. On the contrary it is the product of the whole organization. Consciousness is a very complex and unstable state, consisting of many half-conscious and sub-conscious feelings, which in a healthy state of mind are focused in the present object of attention.

The whole organism with its structures and forms, in so far as we consider its psychical side, is called the soul of that organism. Soul, therefore, we define as the psychical aspect of all the organic forms of our body.

Mind is a synonym of soul. However, the word soul is used with special preference when we refer to our emotional life, while mind rather denotes the intellectual activity of the organism. When we speak of spirit, we think of soul-life without having any reference to the bodily forms in which it manifests itself. In the same way we speak of "the spirit of a book" and "the spirit of the age." If "spirit" is supposed to have an independent existence of itself, the word becomes synomynous with "ghost."

We sum up:

Memory is the preservation of psychic forms. From simple sensations it has produced sensory perceptions in well-organized sense-organs, and then from the perceptions of the sense-organs the concepts of the mind. In the further progress of evolution we reach the domain of knowledge represented in abstract ideas with all their rich and varied forms of thought, which lead man into the provinces of science, art, religion, and philosophy.

COGNITION, KNOWLEDGE, AND TRUTH.

COGNITION in its simplest form is the act of feeling a percept to be the same as another percept perceived before. Cognition thus is founded in the relations of our percepts among each other. A single impression cannot as yet constitute cognition; two or several percepts of the same kind are needed in order to feel their identity.

Cognition consists of two elements; it has a subjective and an objective phase. The objective phase is that the object now perceived is the same (or at least in some respect the same) as the object per-·ceived before; and the subjective phase is that it is also felt to be the same. The new percept fitting itself into the form produced in the brain by the former percept, is, in the literal sense of the word, re-cognized: it is cognized again. The condition of knowledge accordingly, in its simplest form, is 'the sameness of two or more percepts.'

Cognition of the higher and more complicated kind remains at bottom the same. It is always the act of recognizing a unity or a sameness in two or several phenomena. Cognition always presupposes a certain stock of experience, and to understand a phenomenon or to explain it means to recognize its identity with other phenomena with which we are familiar. The falling of stones to the ground is a familiar occurrence with us, and to show in how far the motion of the moon about the earth is the same kind of motion as that of the falling stone, only under other conditions, is an explanation of this phenomenon.

Knowledge is the formulated stock of experiences in which we have discovered common features, so that their identity even under different conditions has been and will always again be recognized.

Knowledge in animals is simple in comparison with knowledge in man. Animals easily recognize concrete things and persons, but they are not able to sum up their knowledge in abstract formulas; they cannot name things, they cannot speak, they cannot think in abstract ideas. Man's knowledge rises into the realm of abstract thought where he creates a new world of spiritual existence.   .

The data of the natural sciences are always certain phenomena of which we are aware by sensation. We classify these phenomena so as to embrace them by the same law in innumerable and, in many respects, apparently different processes. Take, for instance, the tiny luminous specks in the nocturnal sky which we as well as many animals perceive by our visual organs. To the animal the stars are meaningless,* to the savage they are mysterious beings of an undiscoverable origin; but the astronomer by the aid of computing, and measuring, and calculating, with the additional help of telescopes, arranges in his mind the phenomena of the starry heaven in such a way as to make of his luminous sensations a well-ordered whole, standing in unison with all the other facts of our experience.

---

* Incidentally may be mentioned, that to the higher animals natural phenomena gain in impressiveness. The monkeys of the Sunda' Isles, we are informed, gather shortly before sunrise in the highest tree-tops and salute the first rays of the rising sun with clamorous shouts.

Abstract ideas, generalizations, and conceptions of natural laws are the most important factors of human existence proper. By the help of abstract thought only has man become man. By the help of abstract thought only can he realize that he is a part of the whole of All-existence: he becomes religious. By the help of abstract thought he can regulate his actions according to maxims of universal applicability, so that he remains in harmony with the cosmical order of the Universe—with God: he becomes a moral being. By the help of abstract thought he can formulate his experiences in the rigid forms of arithmetical, geometrical, mechanical, or logical expressions, so that he comprehends the immanent necessity of the order of nature: he becomes scientific. When he finds that his abstract conceptions, his ideas, are realized in certain regular or characteristic instances, he acquires artistic taste; and when he begins to express his ideas in a visible or audible form, in colors, in sounds, or in words so that his creations represent single instances, incarnations as it were, of his ideas, he becomes an artist,—a painter, a musician, or a poet. If man succeeds in unifying all his knowledge on a scientific basis, so that it is systematized as a unitary conception of world and life and the aim of life, he becomes a philosopher. Thus abstract thought is the basis of all higher, intellectual, human, and humane aspirations. It raises man high above all the rest of animal creation and makes him their master. It is the corner-stone of humanity and produces Religion, Ethics, Science, Art, and Philosophy.

Abstract thoughts do not on the one hand represent absolute existences, nor on the other are they mere air castles; they are built upon the solid ground of reality. The facts of nature are specie and our abstract thoughts are bills which serve to economize the process of an exchange of thought. We must know the exact value in specie of every bill which is in our possession. And if the values of our abstract ideas are not ultimately founded upon the reality of positive facts, they are like bills or drafts for the payment of which there is no money in the bank.

Reality is often identified with material existence, as if matter were an exhaustive term for all that is real. Matter is an abstract; matter of itself, absolute matter, does not exist. Matter cannot even be conceived as real unless it is possessed with some kind of force (or motion, or energy); forceless matter is a non-entity. Further, every single particle of matter must appear in some special form. Formless matter is a nonentity also. Matter, force, and form are abstracts only, which we have made for our own convenience of comprehending the phenomena of the world. Reality itself is one undivided and indivisible whole. The most important abstraction among the three (matter, force, and form), we do not hesitate to say is, neither matter nor force, but form.

Matter is a general conception abstracted from things material; it indicates their property of possessing mass and volume, but excludes all special or individual features of material bodies. At the same time, accordingly, it is an extremely poor and empty concept. Generalizations naturally are the more void, the higher they are. The same may be said of motion as well as of force. Motion means change of place; force signifies that which is productive of a change of place. In order to know matter, we must become familiar with all kinds of matter, and in order to know the forces of nature we must study the natural phenomena, *viz.*, the actual motions that are taking place.

The concept 'form' is not so barren as the generalizations ' matter ' and 'force.' We cannot create new matter, neither can we create new force or motion, but we can create new forms. We can in our mind construct new combinations; and if they have been correctly arranged in our thoughts, they will (when an attempt at their execution is made) be seen to be realizable. The laws of form laid down in the formal sciences (in mathematics, arithmetic, pure logic, etc.), can be ascertained by self-observation. While we create new forms in our mind we evolve the more complex combinations from the simple ones and can thus comprehend them. We can, by methodical generalization, as well as consistent application of generalizations to different cases, exhaust the possibility of instances and thus formulate universal rules.

Form constitutes the order of the world, its cognizability and intelligibility. It imparts to the universe the spirituality of its existence. Form and the changeability of form make evolution possible. The evolution of forms brings sense and meaning into the forces of nature; it affords a direction to their movements and determines the progressive character of all growth. Form, a special kind of form, constitutes mind and human intelligence, and the establishment of the sciences of formal thought is the basis of exact philosophy. Form gives purpose to life and the problem of ethics finds in it its solution.

We now ask that often repeated question of Pilate, "What is truth?" Tradition says that Pilate was a skeptic; like the agnostic of modern days, he did not consider it worth his while to wait for a reply. And the gospel informs us that Jesus did not deign to answer him.

There have been complaints that we never can know 'absolute truth'; and indeed 'absolute truth' is unknowable because such a thing as 'absolute truth' does not exist. Cognition is a relation, and truth, if it has any meaning at all, means true cognition. Therefore the very essence of truth is a relation; and this relation is neither mysterious, nor inscrutable, nor unknowable, nor a profound secret; it can be ascertained perfectly well.

A conception, or a cognizance, or a formula of a number of experiences, or an abstract idea is true if it is in unison with all facts of reality; it is not true if in any way it conflicts with or is contradicted by facts of reality. The facts of reality remain the ultimate data of all our knowledge; truth is the unison of our conception of single facts with the whole system of all facts, and science as well as philosophy is our aspiration to realize the unity of nature

THE FOUNDATION OF MONISM.

THE very nature of cognition, we have learned, is unification, and through cognition our percepts, our concrete concepts, and our abstract ideas arrange themselves into a unitary system of knowledge. We cannot help searching for a unitary conception of the different phenomena, and our mind will never be at ease unless we at least feel convinced that we have found it. The disposition of our mind must thus naturally lead us to a monistic philosophy which attempts to understand all the single phenomena of the universe, as well as the whole of reality, by one universal law or from one all-embracing principle.

The constitution of the human mind, in this way, predisposes man for monism. The want of a unification of knowledge is the *subjective* condition out of which monism originates, but in itself it would have no value if it were not justified by experience. We can construct a monism a priori by pure reason, but must ratify it a posteriori through scientific investigation. The *objective* condition of monism is founded in the character of our actual experiences. All the natural phenomena which ever came within the grasp of human apprehension, were such as conformed directly or at least showed a possibility (if they were but better known) of conforming, by and by, to a unitary law. The regularity of the course of nature, and the rigidity of natural laws indicating their irrefragable

universality, are the objective arguments in favor of
the oneness of the All, as assumed by monism. The
more science has progressed, the more has this truth
of the oneness of nature been corroborated, and we
cannot doubt but that it will be more and more confirmed. It is a κτῆμα ἐς ἀεί—an intellectual possession
of humanity that has come to stay for good.

It will easily be understood that the oneness of nature (the regularity which pervades the universe and
which can be formulated in natural laws—*die Gesetz-
mässigkeit der Natur*), must be considered as the ground
of, or ultimate *raison d'être* for, the principle of oneness which is found in our mind. Our cognition,
with the help of sensation, only mirrors in our consciousness the phenomena of nature in their regularity; so that knowledge in its entirety must become
a systematic representation of the world in our brain.

Knowledge is not a useless efflorescence of the
mind, as has been supposed by some one-sided idealists; nor does it exist for its own sake simply; it serves
the very practical purpose of orientation in this world.
So far as our knowledge reaches, thus far do we intellectually own nature, and can hope to rule its course in
the interest of humanity by accommodating ourselves
and natural events to nature's unalterable laws.

The unitary conception of the world has become a
postulate of science. Indeed the single sciences, each
one in its province, have always worked out and endeavored to verify the principles of monism. Every
fact which seems to contradict the principle of unity
must be, and indeed it is, considered as a problem
until it conforms to it. As soon as it is found to be in
unison with all the other facts the problem is solved.

Monism, being equivalent to consistency, is that

view to realize which almost every philosopher aspires. Dualists, from principle, are inconsistent thinkers; yet even they attempt to construct at least a sham unity of their systems. Thus, supernaturalists look upon matter as a product of mind and materialists, vice versa, upon mind as a product of matter. The latter believe that life was created by dead matter, and the former that an extramundane God, the principle of life, created matter. They cannot help striving after a monistic view of the world; for the unification of all knowledge is the inherent principle of cognition.

Dualism appears to be a state of transition. It emerges from the more chaotic state of many single unifications of knowledge, that were systematized under two opposite and apparently contradictory principles. Plutarch says in his book, *De Iside et Osiride*, chap. 45:

"The world is neither thrown about by wild chance without intelligence, reason, and guidance, nor is it dominated and directed by one rational being with a rudder or with gentle and easy reins as it were; but on the contrary, there are in it several different things, and those made up of bad as well as good; or rather (to speak more plainly) Nature produces nothing here but what is mixed and tempered. There is not, as it were, one store-keeper, who out of two different casks dispenses to us human affairs adulterated and mixed together,* as a landlord doth his liquors; but by reason of two contrary origins and opposite powers—whereof the one leads to the right hand and in a direct line, and the other turns to the contrary hand and goes athwart—both human life is mixed, and the world (if not all, yet that part which is about the earth and below the moon) is become very unequal and various, and liable to all manner of changes. For if nothing can come without

* Plutarch alludes to Homer, who feigns Jupiter to have in his house two differing jars, the one filled with good things, and the other with bad. See Il. XXIV. 527.

a cause, and if a good thing cannot afford a cause of evil, Nature then must certainly have a peculiar source and origin of evil as well as of good."

Good and evil, light and darkness, heat and cold, appear, at first sight only, as contradictory principles. As soon as we grow more familiar with the facts which we comprehend by these names, and when we attempt to reduce them to exact expressions by measuring their degrees, we perceive that, in reality, they are one and the same principle which can be viewed from opposite standpoints. After the invention of the thermometer the dualism of heat and cold was abolished forever, and a monistic view is firmly established on the basis of exact data, expressed in figures. Every dualism is, upon principle, an inconsistency of thought; but it will peacefully die away as soon as the illogical character of its inconsistency is discovered.

Monism is different from the other philosophical views in so far as it is not so much a finished system, but a plan for a system. It admits of constant realization and further perfection, in all the many branches of knowledge. The plan, however, can be sketched in outline and we need not fear of its being overthrown by unexpected discoveries. Other systems, as a rule, set out with objective principles to which their upholders try to adjust the facts of reality. Some hypothesis is formed and facts are interpreted by this hypothesis. Monism, however, is a subjective principle, a rule informing us how to unify knowledge out of our experiences, a plan how to proceed in building our conception of world and life from facts. We need fear no collision between our pet theories and facts, for it is a matter of principle that we have to take our stand on facts. Monism in this sense, *i. e.*, the formal principle of unity, is the only true philosophy, and we can repeat of monism the same words that Kant said of his Criticism: "The danger is not that of being refuted but merely that of being misunderstood."

FORM AND FORMAL THOUGHT.

I.

KANT'S CRITIQUE OF PURE REASON.

In the introduction to his "Critique of Pure Reason," Immanuel Kant proposes the question: How are synthetical judgments *a priori* possible? On the solution of this problem the whole structure of his philosophy rests, which he characterizes as *Transcendental Idealism.*

'A priori' means ' beforehand,' and its opposite ' a posteriori ' means 'afterwards.' To know something a priori means to know something before any experience thereof has been had. When we know that the specific gravity of ebony is greater than that of water, we can declare a priori, that ebony will not float, but sink to the bottom (the physical law being also considered known). We can even know it *before* the experiment is made. The experiment will afterwards, *i. e.* a posteriori, verify our knowledge.

This is the general meaning of the terms ' a priori ' and ' a posteriori.' But Kant uses the words in a more limited sense.

In Kant's language the term 'experience' is employed to signify sense-perception. It is not exactly limited to that meaning throughout, but certainly it is always used in opposition to non-sensory or

mere formal knowledge. That which produces experience, and which as a reality outside of us and independent of our sensation corresponds to sensory impressions, Kant calls 'matter.' Therefore, we have
knowledge of the existence of matter and its different
properties 'a posteriori,' or from experience, *i. e.* from
sense-perception only.

There is another kind of knowledge, however, which
is not sense-knowledge, but formal knowledge. Formal
knowledge can be gained by abstraction. The form of
things, such as globes, cubes, statues, and other bodies,
can be abstracted from their material reality. We can,
for instance, think away all things in the world. (We
abstract from their material existence.) What is left is
'empty space'; and this conception of pure space is the
postulate of a science that is called mathematics.
We can abstract, also, from all processes which take
place in the world; what is left is the idea of duration
only; it is 'empty time,' in which these processes
might have taken place. The conception of time, pure
and simple, can be conceived as a progress through
empty units without reference to real phenomena.
Such empty units are called numbers, and by adding
one unit to another, we start a process that is known
as counting. Counting is the basis of arithmetic. If,
again, we abstract from the substance of our thoughts,
the mere forms of thought remain, which, treated as a
science, are called formal logic.

It must be remarked in passing that Kant calls
space and time 'pure perceptions' (*reine Anschauun-
gen*), while the categories are treated as 'pure conceptions' (*reine Verstandesbegriffe*). This distinction
is justifiable for certain purposes, and should not be
slurred over by commentators of Kant's philosophy.

However, our present purpose is not to explain or popularize the Critique of Pure Reason, but to use its more prominent ideas for propounding our own views which grew out of a study of Kant's Transcendentalism. We may add that every perception, as soon as it is named and clearly defined, becomes a conception. Space can be the basis of mathematics, and time of arithmetic only when both have grown to be clear conceptions.

Formal knowledge is called by Kant a priori, because, if any truth of these formal sciences is established, it will be known to be true for all possible cases of experience, even before the experiments have been made. The rules of mathematics, of arithmetic, and logic, possess rigid necessity and absolute universality. They are the condition of all scientific investigation; for rigidity and universality (*Nothwendigkeit und Allgemeinheit*) in experimental sciences can be realized only through the assistance of the formal sciences. Astronomy and chemistry, for instance, have become sciences only by the application of mathematics and arithmetic; and where can any kind of science be found that could dispense with logic?

A priori, as used in the limited sense by Kant, is purely formal knowledge, while a posteriori is identical with experience. Marks of a priori truths are, according to Kant, absolute rigidity and universality (*Nothwendigkeit und Allgemeinheit*).

Kant has been represented as a philosopher who teaches by his doctrine of the a priori, that man has innate ideas ready in his consciousness. Pure reason, he was supposed to believe, wells up in us as some mysterious power coming from trandescendent and most probably supernatural regions. This is absolutely unfounded, as can be learned from the very first sentence in the introduction to his "Critique of Pure Reason":

> " *That all our knowledge begins with experience there can be no*
> " *doubt.* For how is it possible that the faculty of cognition should
> " be awakened into exercise otherwise than by means of objects
> " which affect our senses, and partly of themselves produce repre-
> " sentations, partly rouse our powers of understanding into activity,
> " to compare, to connect, or to separate these, and so to convert
> " the raw material of our sensory impressions into a knowledge of
> " objects, which is called experience? * *In respect of time, there-*
> " *fore, no knowledge of ours is antecedent to experience, but begins*
> " *with it.*"

In order to show that formal knowledge must be distinguished from sensory experience, Kant continues:

> " But, though all our knowledge begins with experience, it by
> " no means follows, that all arises out of experience.† For, on the
> " contrary, it is quite possible that our empirical knowledge is a
> " compound of that which we receive through impressions, and
> " that which the faculty of cognition supplies from itself (sensory
> " impressions giving merely the occasion), an addition which we
> " cannot distinguish from the original element given by sense, till
> " long practice has made us attentive to, and skillful in, separating
> " it. It is, therefore, a question which requires close investiga-
> " tion, and is not to be answered at first sight—whether there ex-
> " ists a knowledge altogether independent of experience, and even
> " of all sensory impressions? Knowledge of this kind is called a
> " priori, in contradistinction to empirical knowledge, which has its
> " sources a posteriori, that is, in experience."

Formal knowledge is independent of sensory experience in so far as we purposely exclude all sensory experience. But, after all, inasmuch as sensory experience is the beginning of all knowledge, a posteriori as well as a priori, to that extent formal

---

* The word ' experience ' is here used in the popular acceptation, being taken as the result of sensory impressions fashioned by pure thought.

† Here the word is used in the limited sense, as sensory experience.

knowledge is dependent upon sensory experience (as Kant emphatically declares). Experience is antecedent in time, and from it alone formal knowledge can originate, which—not until a certain height of mental development has been reached — will be separated from the raw material of sensory impressions.

Kant, using the word experience in the limited sense of sensory experience, declares that investigation must go beyond experience in order to find the laws of formal knowledge, or pure thought. He, therefore, called all formal knowledge transcendental, and speaks of transcendental logic, transcendental dialectic, transcendental mathematics, and transcendental arithmetic.

Transcendental is by no means transcendent. Transcendent means unknowable, or what transcends knowledge; transcendental, according to Kant, means what transcends experience. It is not unknowable, but, on the contrary, the basis of all knowledge, and the transcendental sciences treat such subjects as demand (if treated with accuracy) axiomatic certainty. The mysterious has no place in the realms of the transcendental.

The question 'How are synthetical judgments a priori possible?' is to the same purpose as another question of Kant's, propounded in his Prolegomena, § 36, where he asks: "How is nature possible?" When Kant speaks of nature, he refers to our conception of reality, in so far as it is, or can become, the object of science representing the cosmical order of nature. We do not now intend to enter into the details of the problem, as to how far we agree with the sage of Königsberg, and how far we do not agree. But it seems necessary to point out the importance of the problem, on the solution of which the possibility of scientific knowledge depends.

The faculty of thinking *in abstracto* is called reason; and reason (which on earth man alone possesses by virtue of language) can become the basis of science, if by a critical method fallacies and vagaries of reason are prevented. Kant says in the introduction to his " Critique of Pure Reason : "

> " The critique of reason leads at last, naturally and neces-
> " sarily, to science; and, on the other hand, the dogmatical use of
> " reason without criticism leads to groundless assertions, against
> " which others equally specious can always be set, thus ending un-
> " avoidably in skepticism."

The whole book is devoted to this critique. It shows that pure reason (formal thought) is limited to formal truths only and cannot contain revelations as to the substantial (the sensory or material) contents of our conceptions. This should have been self-evident; but as a matter of fact, philosophers before and even after Kant have most confidently asserted much about God and the world, the human soul, innate ideas, and other things, while their whole reasoning rested upon unwarranted a priori arguments. Such philosophers Kant calls dogmatical. Wolf (1679-1754), who had most methodically systematized the metaphysical doctrines of his time, is the most representative dogmatic philosopher.

If we compare our cognition to building material, Kant said, our transcendental knowledge has been employed by dogmatical philosophers for erecting a lofty dome that should reach to Heaven. For this purpose the " Critique of Pure Reason " has found the materials insufficient. Nevertheless, our transcendental cognition is most valuable; certainly it is unfit for the airy castles of supernatural systems; but if employed for its proper purpose, Kant continues, "it very well suffices for a mansion here on earth spacious enough for all our purposes and high enough to enable us to survey the level plain of experience."

Formal cognitions, or conceptions a priori, are of themselves "empty;" and sensory impressions of themselves are "blind." If we had only unconnected sensory impressions, we would be worse off than the lowest animalcula or even plants, and the materials of our experience received through our sensory organs would be of no avail. Our formal cognitions furnish the mortar, as it were, of a synthetic method which will enable us to arrange sensory impressions in comprehensively arranged systems. Formal cognition and sensory experience, therefore, are the warp and woof of scientific knowledge. The warp as well as the woof, each by itself, consists of single threads, but in their combination they will furnish a well-woven fabric.

If a philosopher limits his method to sensory experience alone, he will never attain scientific certainty; he can never make definite and positive statements, but will only propose *opinions* which may be overturned on the slightest occasion. Such a one-sided empirical, or naturalistic, philosopher would be guilty of the opposite error of the dogmatist, and while the dogmatist ultimately must arrive at futile assertions, the empiricist's mere opinions must lead directly to skepticism. As the representative philosopher of skepticism, Kant mentions David Hume. David Hume does not recognize the difference between formal knowledge and sensory experience. To him, therefore, all knowledge consists of single, unconnected threads of knowledge.

On the last two pages of Kant's "Critique of Pure Reason," we read the following passages:

"We may divide the methods at present employed in the field "of enquiry into the naturalistic and the scientistic."

'Naturalistic' here means what is commonly called "common sense philosophy," which, repudiating all speculation, does not feel the need of a critical method. Kant continues:

"The naturalist of pure reason lays it down as his principle, " that common reason, without the aid of science—which he calls " "sound reason, or common sense—can give a more satisfactory " answer to the most important questions of metaphysics than spec- "ulation is able to do. He must maintain, therefore, that we can "determine the content and circumference of the moon more " certainly by the naked eye than by the aid of mathematical rea- "soning. But this system is mere misology [contempt of rational " thought] reduced to principles; and, what is the most absurd " thing in this doctrine, the neglect of all scientific means is paraded " as a peculiar method of extending our cognition. As regards " those who are naturalists because they know no better, they are " certainly not to be blamed. They follow common sense, with- " out parading their ignorance as a method which is to teach us the " wonderful secret, how we are to find the truth which lies at the " bottom of the well of Democritus."

'Scientistic' denotes here the method of one-sided scientists. The original German text reads *scienti-fisch*, which has been coined by Kant in opposition to *wissenshaftslich, i. e.* scientific in its usual sense. This scientistic, or one-sided scientific, method lacks critique; it does not distinguish between formal and sensory (between a priori and a posteriori), and must either undervalue the importance of formal cognition, by not properly employing it as a synthetic principle, or overvalue the importance of formal cognition by attributing to it the power of a supernatural revelation. Kant continues, and concludes his "Critique of Pure Reason" as follows:

"As regards those who wish to pursue a scientistic method, they
" have now the choice of following either the dogmatical or the
'skeptical, while they are bound never to desert the systematic
"mode of procedure.   When I mention, in relation to the former,
" the celebrated Wolf, and as regards the latter, David Hume, I
" may leave, in accordance with my present intention, all others
" unnamed.

"The critical path alone is still open. If my reader has
" been kind and patient enough to accompany me on this hith-
" erto untraveled route, he can now judge whether, if he and oth-
" crs will contribute their exertions towards making this narrow
" foot-path a high-road of thought, that, which many centuries
" have failed to accomplish, may not be executed before the close
" of the present—namely, to bring Reason to perfect contentment
" in regard to that which has always, but without permanent re-
" sults, occupied her powers and engaged her ardent desire for
" knowledge."

II.

THE ORIGIN OF THE 'A PRIORI.'

KANT answers the question 'How are synthetic
judgments a priori possible?' by showing that such
synthetic judgments undoubtedly exist.

A synthetic judgment is different from an analytic
judgment.   An analytic judgment merely analyses
knowledge and contains nothing but an explanation or
elucidation of what, in an involved form, we have
known before, but a synthetic judgment really ampli-
fies our knowledge; it adds to the stock of our knowledge something new, which we have not known before.   In proving that the exterior angle of a triangle
is equal to the sum of the two opposite interior angles
of the same, we amplify our knowledge of the triangle
by mere ratiocination, a priori. Kant uses even a simpler instance. The judgment $7 + 5 = 12$ is not analytic

but synthetic. The concept twelve is neither contained in seven nor in five, but is something entirely
new.

Kant leaves the subject here and is satisfied with
the fact *that* synthetic judgments a priori are possible.
He might have ventured a step further by pro-
posing another question: 'What is the origin of the
a priori?' Only by answering this question could he
have shown, *how* synthetic judgments a priori are
possible. This he did not do, and the omission has
produced great confusion among German, French,
and English thinkers.

The word 'a priori' is undoubtedly an old-fash-
ioned and awkward expression, which has not yet lost
the savor of 'innate ideas.' It was readily accepted in
England by philosophers of a theological bias who
were little aware of the dangerous properties concealed
in this Kantian idea. It sounds so scholarly Latin,
almost ecclesiastical; for it is an expression handed
down from mediæval times. But when they drew this
clumsy wooden horse within the walls of their dogmatic stronghold, they unwittingly admitted an army
of bellicose warriors—Kant's critical thoughts—who
are sure to conquer and destroy the citadel of dualistic
orthodoxy.

"The old fashioned a priori in science, in morals,
and religion," a reviewer in *Science** somewhere remarks "used to be represented as an arrogant and in-
tolerant thing, mysterious in its manner of speech, vi-
olent and dogmatic in the defense of its own claims.
The English Empiricists used to hate this aristocratic
a priori and they shrewdly suspected it to be a humbug. What they gave us in its place, however, was a

---

*Science. Vol. V, p. 202.

vague and unphilosophic doctrine of science that you could only seem to understand so long as you did not examine into its meaning." J. S. Mill's philosophy moved in a circle. "He had founded all inductive interpretation of nature on the causal principle and the causal principle again on an inductive interpretation of nature."

Kant, as we have stated, calls the a priori truths 'formal knowledge,' and this indicates that the general postulates of the transcendental sciences, the axiomatic conceptions from which they start, are abstracted from reality by thinking away, as it were, their material existence, which is represented in our sensory impressions. Kant suggests this conception of the a priori, but he nowhere pronounces it. On the contrary, he makes statements which may be taken to exclude this interpretation of his conception.

According to our view, form is a property of reality as well as of our cognition. Formless matter does not exist. Form and matter, as they exist in reality, are inseparable. What is called formless matter is either uniform or lacking that kind of form which, in our opinion or according to our wishes, it should have. Knowledge also in its primitive shape, when it is, so to say, natural and crude, is an intimate combination of sense-perceptions and formal cognition. The sense-perceptions are the real substance of knowledge, while formal cognition is the principle which arranges and systematizes sense-experience.

As soon as a living being develops the ability to think *in abstracto*, a state which is attained by means of language, he can think of different qualities independent of things. He can think of whiteness, of greatness, of smallness, of courage, and of cowardice. And soon after that, he will be also able to think one, two, three, four, five units *in abstracto* without the assistance of his fingers; he will count. Counting is a most important step in the development of humanity, for it is the first purely formal thought. It abstracts from the objects counted and refers exclusively to the unit numbers which then may be employed for any kind of things.

Physiologically considered the growth of abstract and formal ideas must have developed in the following way:

Irritations in the amœba can only produce vague feelings. Light and darkness, heat and cold, moisture and aridity, abundance and scarcity of food, exercise a certain influence upon the animalcule; they act upon it in a certain way and produce more or less favorable or unfavorable effects in the living substance which may ultimately result in reactions of some kind. In higher animals irritations are reacted upon differently in different organs. Sensitiveness has been differentiated, and a ray of light is perceived on the nerves of the skin as warmth and in those of the eye as light.

The same process of differentiation and specialization takes place in the brain. If a horse is seen, its image appears on the retina of the eye, whence the irritation is transmitted through the optic nerve to the interior parts of the brain. There it is perceived as a horse. According to Hering[*] and other physiologists, there is no doubt but that every new perception of a horse is registered on the same spot in the brain as previously. Every single brain-cell has a memory of its own, which makes it more fit to be irritated by

---

[*] See Ewald Hering; Memory as a General Function of Organized Matter THE OPEN COURT, p. 143.

that perception to which it has adapted itself. Thus, the conception of a horse is the sum total of all percepts of a horse. It is, as Mr. Hegeler * most appropriately expresses it, like a composite photograph. The common features of a certain group of same things are preserved, while the individual traits become blurred and are lost sight of.

Thus the many varying images of the eye, and all sensory impressions, as well as motory exertions, are registered somewhere in the brain, each kind in its place. The special memory of the different fibres and cells naturally arranges all percepts and concepts in a proper order. Moreover, a repeated simultaneousness of different sensations which are produced by same causes in different sense-organs, produces associations between certain percepts. We think of the rose and at the same time of its smell and its color. We see a bird and think of his song, and the dog who sees the whip feels at once in his recollection the pain caused by its lash.

Horses have been perceived which are different in size, and color, and temper, etc. These differences are occasionally of importance. A horse may attract attention because it is as white as snow. The horse is perceived and also its whiteness. Thus a new concept is created, the concept of a quality which does

---

* Mr. E. C. Hegeler, in his essay, "The Soul," (see THE OPEN COURT, p. 393) says:

" If an abstraction is made, many things having something in common are put together, and what they have in common is specified in words. It is then forgotten that what they do not have in common disappears in the generalization. The same takes place in Galton's composite photographs of the members of a family. Only that remains of the several faces what they have in common. This implies that the composite photograph is entirely contained in each of the single photographs of each member, each is the complete composite with additions. So in reality the composite photograph is an abstraction—a part—of each of the single photographs."

not correspond to, but has been abstracted from, concrete objects. White roses, white snow, white stones (as lime or chalk), and white horses have been perceived, and the percept of 'whiteness' is produced, to which again a special province of the brain must be ascribed, which of course must be connected by nerve fibres with all white things, more so with things that are always white than with those that appear so only occasionally. The psychical connection of such concepts is called association.

Suppose we are in a library where the books are well arranged by a number of librarians who have different but each one his own special interests. Many books are being constantly delivered. There are books about horses, and dogs, and flowers, and stones, etc., etc. Every librarian takes the books of that subject with whose study he is specially engaged and places it in his alcove. The library would be in the best order, and yet so long as the different alcoves were not named, most of its treasures would be inaccessible for many most important purposes. Such is the arrangement in animal brains. A dog knows what a cat is. Every new perception of a cat awakens in his mind with more or less vividness all the many previous percepts of a cat with their different associations, mostly memories of pursuit, perhaps also of resistance and combat. But all these memories are single percepts. They have not yet coalesced into a unitary and clear conception of catdom. If the sum total of the cat-percepts in his memory is to be called a conception, it is certainly a very imperfect kind of conception. A conception becomes distinct only by being named. This is the truth which has been so splendidly elucidated by our best philological authorities, namely, that thought (the abstract thought of reasonable beings) is only possible by the help of language. Man thinks because he speaks. The name of a thing is, as it were, a string tied around all the many percepts of that thing, thus comprehending them all in one concept. Concept is derived from *con* and *capio* and means, according to its etymology, a taking or grasping together, a gathering into and holding in one.

The act of naming is therefore an enormous economy in mental activity; it is the mechanical means by which abstract ideas or generalizations are formed; and the faculty of thinking *in abstracto* is called reason. Reason, therefore, in its elementary origin, is abstracting and combining. Abstracting is a kind of separation. We separate the quality of white from white objects and combine all the different white-sensations into one concept by the name of 'whiteness.' *Both* processes, that of separation and of combination, are essential features of reason; but they are *the* essential features, and all functions of reason can be reduced to these two processes.*

Our brain is like a workshop in full and unceasing activity. In its operation, we must distinguish three things:

---

* F. Max Müller defines Reason as "addition and subtraction." We have repeatedly given our full assent to the great philologist's views with the remark, that we should substitute for "addition and subtraction" the terms used above, *i. e.*, "combination and separation." The terms "addition and subtraction" are confined to arithmetic; and to our mind they are different from "combination and separation" in so far as "subtraction" is used of units that are taken away from other equal units, while "separation" takes a part from something that appeared as a unit (an integral whole) before the separation. Similarly an addition sums up units of the same kind (or at least those which for the purpose of addition are considered as being of the same kind) into a larger number, while a combination unites parts into one consolidated whole. We believe that there is no substantial difference between Prof. Max Müller's view and our own.

1. The activity which is called life; it is a special kind of energy. Its presence makes itself felt as motion, which is a change of place and could be, if all details were known, mechanically expressed.

2. The material of which the whole workshop of the brain consists, and which is used to keep it in working order; viz., the matter which is constantly combining and decomposing in the protoplasm of the brain-substance.

3. The form in which life operates in the nervous substance. Every brain-cell has a special form, the groups of cells are arranged in special forms and the whole system of the different cerebral organs is built up in a special form.

We distinguish these three things, but in reality they are inseparably united. If our percepts and concepts are to be physically considered, they should not be represented as the activity only of the brain, nor as brain-substance, nor as their mere form. They are activity, and matter, and form united; being a special form of the activity in brain-substance. It goes without saying that the form of a special energy depends upon the form of that substance in which the process takes place. The form of a motion and the form of the substance in which the motion takes place, are not only interdependent, they are identical.

A certain percept, being a special form of motion in living brain substance, leaves in those cells in which it takes place, such vestiges as to produce a disposition adapted not only to receive the same or similar percepts, but even to reproduce that percept spontaneously, if the cells, nourished by the blood-circulation, are stimulated into activity through some inner process by association. This disposition (called by Hering *Stimmung*, which is produced by the special memory of organized matter), becomes stronger by repetition and thus imparts more and more stability to that special form.

Physiologically considered, percepts and concepts are very complicated structures which in their associations may resemble a kind of three-dimensional network, showing interlacings of innumerable star-shaped knots, the threads of which interradiate and combine the various sensory percepts belonging to the same idea. But for the sake of simplicity let us suppose that perceptions and conceptions grew in a brain like cells and groups of cells simply; they would naturally and mechanically arrange themselves in systematic order. One of the first steps in the evolution of living matter is that of giving stability to its outer form by enveloping itself in a membrane. Form, as we understand the term, is not only the outside shape, but also the inner disposition and arrangement of atoms. However, for the sake of simplicity again, and as a matter of crude illustration, let us for a moment use the membranes of cells as an example of their forms. The membranes of cells are also organic substance and their material particles are constantly changing. Nevertheless, they possess a relative stability which represents the shape of the cells, *i. e.*, their outer form. If we would take out of such a brain the living substance without destroying the membranes in which the cells have enveloped themselves, it would afford an aspect of divisions and subdivisions not unlike that of the departments, shelves, and pigeon holes of a library from which the books are removed, and we would have an anatomical representation of a system of formal thought.

It is understood that this explanation is a simile only to show that form grows *pari passu* with its substance, and mere form, if abstracted from its substance, is, for purposes of thought, by no means valueless; it is of greatest importance for a proper orientation among the enormous mass of sense-perceptions that crowd upon the mind.

An animal and a man may have the very same sensory impressions; their brain substance consists of the same combinations of nervous matter; sensations (the basis of all mental activity) are produced by the same kind of organs and in the same way. Yet there is a difference of form between the animal and the human brain in so far as the many different impressions · of same percepts have not yet attained in the animal brain that stability and unity which they possess in the human brain. In the human brain the subdivisions are more marked, the furrows are deeper as well as more numerous; and from recent investigations we know that every class of same perceptions has acquired an additional and closely associated brain structure which embodies its name.* The whole group of certain percepts together with their name represents what in logical and psychological language is called a concept.

Let us now suppose that the chief librarian of the library of our brains for the sake of arranging a catalogue takes an inventory of all the books arranged in the different alcoves. He would find the same principle of arrangement applied everywhere. The differ-

---

* Compare the map and explanations of the human brain in *Der Mensch*, by Dr. Johannes Ranke, Vol. I, p. 530 et seq. The chapter, "*Lokalisation in der Grauen Grosshirnrinde*," explains Broca's, Hitzig's, and Fritsch's investigations. It takes into consideration the arguments proposed by adversaries of the localization theory (Goltz, etc.), and adopts Exner's view which, it appears, reconciles seemingly irreconcilable principles.

ent alcoves would have separate departments and these
again would be found to possess subdivisions. This
kind of arrangement, which, as we stated above, grew
naturally, became first apparent when the process of
naming took place. Many different names were conceived in our consciousness to be special kinds of one
general kind so that they together formed one system
of ideas. Logicians call it *genera* and *species*.

The librarian (we now suppose) arranges an office
(perhaps for the purpose of reference) in which a general plan of the whole library can be found. This reference room contains no books. The visitor finds there
no substantial information; the information to be
gained there is purely formal and serves the purpose
to find one's way easier in the many different departments of the alcoves. This reference room in our brain
is called logical ability, or mathematical reasoning, or
calculation, and we need not say that its establishment
marks another important step in the development of
reason; it is formal thought. It is the beginning of
scientific thought by the help of which we gain information about the methodical arrangement of our
conceptions. Logic does not create order and system
in our brain, but it makes us conscious of the order
that naturally grew in our mind.

The difference between the library and our mind
is, that in a library the shelves have been put up before the books were stored, but in our brains the
different notions form (or rather grow) their own
categories. The notions of our minds are like living
books that build their own shelves and pigeon-holes,
similar to the way in which cellulizing protoplasm
covers itself spontaneously with a membrane. If we
abstract from the protoplasm, which constitutes the

contents of cells, we retain the empty membranes, and if we abstract from the sensory material of percepts and concepts, we retain their mere forms, which, re-duced to rule, are called formal thought, *i. e.,* arith-metic, mathematics, mechanics, and logic.

Knowledge of objects has been gained by sensory impressions, but knowledge of logic can be acquired only by a process of self-observation. It is a kind of internal experience which is quite different from that of external experience; the latter takes place by, and can never dispense with, the instrumentality of the senses. If the rules of pure logic are to be established, we must carefully exclude from this process of inner self-contemplation the interference of the senses, for it is only the form of things, and thoughts, and mo-tions, with which in purely formal thought we are con-cerned. The importance of these forms becomes at once apparent if we bear in mind that as they are in one case they must be in all others also. The rules by which we generalize our knowledge of formal con-ditions (of mathematics, arithmetic, logic and mechan-ics) possess universality and necessity.

The process of scientific enquiry will be seen to be everywhere the same. Science classifies sensory ex-perience according to the categories of formal thought. In so far as we succeed in reducing the data of a certain subject to mechanical, mathematical, arithmetical, or logical principles, we solve its problems and recognize why the different phenomena which are subject to our special enquiry *must* be such as they are. Science traces necessity everywhere; and science can do so only by the help of the formal truths, which, holding good for all imaginable cases, show single instances under the aspect of universal and irrefragable rules.

III.

THE ORDER OF NATURE.

FORMAL thought represents the mere laws of thought in their abstractness, and has been acquired by abstraction. The mere forms of thought exhibit a wonderful regularity which excites our admiration all the more from the great advantages man derives from it. This regularity of formal thought, which is expressed in all logical laws, arithmetical calculations, and in all mathematical conceptions, has naturally grown in our mind as the psychical expression of a physical regularity in the arrangement of the various brain-structures and their combinations.

The arrangement of brain-structures in certain regular forms has been effected in accordance with the same laws that govern the development of forms generally. Therefore, the problem "why man happens to be a logical and reasonable being," turns out to be the same as that "why are the cells in plants arranged in a certain order?" and as that "why do crystals possess a certain regularity?" The problem common in these three questions is: "Why is the world a cosmos (an orderly arranged whole) and not a chaos?" It is the same problem that Kant proposed when he asked: "How is Nature possible at all?"

The problem has been solved differently by different philosophers, and there is no mark that better characterizes a philosophy than the answer it proposes as an explanation of the order of the world. Supernaturalism says: The order of the world is due to a special ukase of a Creator. Materialism, on the other hand, declares that order is the product of chance. Both views have much more in common than appears at first sight. Materialism and supernaturalism are antagonistic and their explanations are irreconcilable. Nevertheless, both start from the same supposition which, from the monistic standpoint, appears to be erroneous: both are dualistic in so far as they consider the world as one thing, and order as another. Order, they declare, has been imposed upon the world either by a transcendent legislator or by a blind chance. Supernaturalism teaches that in the beginning there was *tohuvabhohu*, 'the earth was without form and void,' and materialism similarly begins the history of the world with chaos.

Theological dogmatists anthropomorphize God to such an extent that they compare him to a watchmaker, and the world to a watch. The order of the world, they imagine, has been fashioned to his designs. It is not in itself necessary, but posited by his will. It is necessary only in so far as his intention makes it so. On the other hand, materialistic thinkers similarly explain the order of the world, if not as the result of a wilful act, yet as the fortuitous outcome of blind chance. One of them expresses his opinion as follows: "The first elements, after testing every kind of position and production possible by their mutual unions, at length settled in the form and way they now present."

In opposition to both views, the monistic conception considers the world as a cosmos, *i. e.* an orderly arranged whole. Monism says: "The world and the phenomena of the world are orderly arranged, according to mechanical laws."

Consider how many billions of other combinations of the atoms in an amœba are possible, or at

least thinkable! And nature should have tried all
these infinite possibilities, or part of them, before creating the amœba, and then the hydra, and then the
worm, and so forth! Oh no! The order of the world
is no hap-hazard effect, it is no fortuitous outcome of
chaos. *There is no chaos and never has been a chaos.*
Even in the gaseous nebula there is order and law,
and it appears as chaos only in comparison to the
more evolved state of a planetary system. Thus the
barbaric stage of savage life appears to us as lacking
in social order; and our present state of civilization, it
is to be hoped, will appear to future generations as the
chaos out of which their better arranged society
emerged.

Kant says on this subject: "The aforementioned
expositors of the mechanical theory of cosmic genesis
(Epicurus, Leucippus, and Lucretius) derived every
arrangement perceptible in the cosmic system from
fortuitous accident, which caused the atoms so to hit
together that they made up a well-ordered whole. Epicurus, indeed, was so presumptuous, as to require the
atoms to swerve from their direct motion without any
cause at all, in order to be able to meet one another.
Every one of these philosophers carried this nonsensical
principle so far, as to ascribe the origin of all animate
creatures to this same blind concurrence of atoms, and
actually derived reason from what is not reason (*Ver-
nunft* from *Unvernunft*). In my system of science, on
the contrary, I discover matter joined to certain necessary laws. In its complete dissolution and disper-
sion I see a beautiful and orderly whole naturally
arising. This does not occur through accident or at
hap-hazard, but it is seen that natural properties
necessarily bring it about." Kant argues that this ne-

cessary order is a proof of the existence of God. We argue from our standpoint that this order is due to the laws of form. It can be ascertained and comprehended by an application of the laws of formal thought. This order produces, on the one hand, the *intelligibility* of the world and, on the other, the *intelligence* of rational beings. In its highest stage this order appears as a moral law to which rational beings voluntarily conform so as to be in unison with the whole cosmos. This order, we maintain, is immanent in the universe and, in fact, *it is God.* Human reason mirrors this order in the sentient brain of a living being and thus the sacred legend is justified in declaring that man has been created in the image of God.

The laws of order are omnipresent and eternal. The omnipresence and eternity of these laws does not denote transcendency, or unknowability, or supernaturalness. Nothing of the kind! It simply means that as they are in one case, so are they rigidly in all others. In their most simple shape, the laws of formal thought (logical, arithmetical, mathematical, etc. rules) are recognized as self-evident and necessary, so that we attribute to them absolute certainty and universality. The more complicated processes of higher algebra, higher mathematics, or highly involved logical ratiocinations, appear less absolute to those who are not familiar with abstract reasoning, but are after all just as absolute. We are, by reason of their complexity, liable to be easily mistaken, but, errors on our part excluded, they in themselves are quite as certain and universal, rigid and necessary, as those simple rules which are generally accepted as axioms.

Kant solves the problem " How is Nature possible at all? " in the following way. The highest or most

general laws of Nature, he argues, are within us and
can be stated a priori, independent of sensory experience.   He thinks it is a strange and wonderful fact
that our formal thought (the rules of arithmetic,
mathematics, logic, etc., which are a priori) agrees so
precisely with the highest (i. e., the most general)
laws of nature, which can be ascertained and verified
a posteriori by experience.   Kant sees only two ways
of solution.   Either the laws of pure reason, he says,
have been gathered by experience from nature, or, on
the contrary, the laws of nature have been deduced
from our a priori rules.   The former solution is impossible, since the formal sciences are proven to have been
formulated with the exclusion of all sensory experience.
"Therefore," says Kant, "the second solution only remains.   Reason dictates its laws to Nature"; *i. e.*
our reason is so constituted that it conceives everything in the forms of space, time, and the categories
of pure reason.   Space, time, and the categories are
a part of the thinking subject, which cannot but think
in these forms, and must thus transfer them to the
objects.   Our surroundings affect us by what we
call sensory impressions.   The sensory impressions
are the raw material only from which the well-ordered
whole of nature, as an object of science, is created by
the synthetic faculty of reason.   Reason with the help
of formal thought shapes this intellectual world in our
minds, which is, so to say, projected outside of ourselves into our surroundings.

Kant has taken into consideration two ways only.
He overlooked the third and most obvious explanation.   His explanation, therefore, will be seen to be
one-sided and insufficient. The third possibility is that
which has been propounded in the foregoing pages.

According to our explanation, the formal (the highest or most general) laws of Nature and the formal laws of thought are identical. Their agreement is not wonderful but inevitable as both are expressions of the forms of existence in general.

Kant's explanation is *one-sided*, beçause if the formal laws of Nature have been dictated by the thinking subject, it does not explain why the formal thought (our knowledge, a priori) is so precisely verified by experience. If we see, as it were, the order *into* nature, how is it that this imposition upon nature is not frustrated? Nature is by no means pliant to any fictitious dictation of subjective laws a priori. It frustrates incorrect a priori reasoning; but tallies with correct and exact calculations. Therefore we conclude, that the form of nature is the same as that of our reason. The forms of thought agree with the forms of existence for the reason that the forms of thought are only a special kind of the forms of existence.

Kant's explanation is, further, *insufficient;* it does not explain how formal thought originates. And this insufficiency of Kant's explanation, we believe, has given rise to many errors. This gap in Kant's philosophy, we think, has been the place in which mystical followers of Kant have been enabled to construct their ontological or supernatural illusions. The transcendental conceptions of pure reason have been declared by them to be of transcendent* origin. The opposition of John Stuart Mill and his school to Kant's conception of the a priori arose, as Mr. Mill confesses in his autobiography, from his considering the transcendental philosophy as an imposition of this kind—an impo-

---

* We have repeatedly called the reader's attention to the difference Kant makes between transcendent (unknowable) and transcendental (formal).

sition by which inveterate beliefs and deep-seated pre-
judices could be consecrated.

According to our solution, the radical difference
obtaining between formal and material (between what
Kant defines as a priori and a posteriori) is not neglected; on the contrary, its fundamental impoitance
is fully recognized and firmly established. The conception of necessity which is the basis of all science,
has found its justification as attaching everywhere to
form—the laws of form being everywhere the same.
The order of the Universe is thus recognized as an
immanent necessity. This necessity can be traced
with the assistance of formal thought everywhere,
as shaping or having shaped the forms of existence. The laws of form being the same everywhere,
our reason can, if not properly dictate, as Kant says,
yet inform us about the form of existence in the
whole universe. The laws of formal thought being
absolutely and universally applicable, are our guide
which like the thread of Ariadne safely leads us through
the labyrinth of the manifold sensory experiences. It
is this method, and this is the only one, which frees
philosophy of mysticism, be it the mysticism of supernaturalists or of agnostics.

IV.

THE BASIS OF THE ECONOMY OF THOUGHT.

MATHEMATICS, as still taught in our schools, is, after
the example of Euclid, unfortunately constructed on
axioms. The introduction of axioms still gives to
mathematics an air of mysteriousness which should be
absent in this most reliable and well established sci-

ence. This doctrinal method of teaching mathematics, by starting from authoritative axioms, which have to be accepted on good faith, is unphilosophical and should give place to a more rational method. It induced Schopenhauer to declare that the whole science, being based upon non-proven truths, remains non-proven. He considers mathematical certainty to be ultimately a part of intuition and thus reaches a point where mysticism can have full play.

Hermann Grassmann in his "theory of extension" (*Ausdehnungslehre*) avoids the faults of Euclid's method. Grassmann throws a new light upon Kant's idea of the a priori by formulating a science of pure mathematics. Our space has three dimensions (*Ausdehnungen*, or extensions), and plane geometry is a mathematics of two dimensions. Grassmann's idea was, to propound mathematics as it would appear if absolutely abstracted from dimensions of any number. This science of pure mathematics must be the most abstract formal thought.*

The "theory of forms in general" (*Allgemeine Formenlehre*), Grassmann says, should precede all the special branches of mathematics. By a theory of forms in general he understands "that series of truths which

*The ingenious attempts of Bolyai and the Russian geometer Lobatschewsky (discussed in C. F. Gauss's 'Briefwechsel mit Schumacher,' Vol. II. pp. 268 to 271), to erect a geometrical system which would be independent of the Euclidian axioms in regard to parallels, and Riemann's meritorious essay " On The Hypotheses Of Geometry," have called the attention of mathematicians and scientists to a remarkable problem which finds its natural and most simple solution in Grassmann's theory of pure mathematics. Hamilton's method of Quaternions is contained in it also, since Grassmann takes into account the length *and direction* of lines. For brief information on the subject see Helmholtz's lucid sketch *Ueber die Thatsachen, die der Geometrie zu Grunde liegen* (Upon the Facts that lie at the Basis of Geometry), J. B. Stallo, "The Concepts and Theories of Modern Physics," pp. 208 seqq., and 248 seqq., and compare also with Hermann Grassmann : *Ausdehnungslehre, Anhang* I. and III. pp. 273 seqq., and 277 seqq.

refers equally to all branches of mathematics and which presupposes only the general concepts of identity and difference, of combination and separation. * * Products of thought can originate in two ways, either by a simple creative act (that of positing) or by the double act of positing and combining. The product of the former kind is a constant form or magnitude in a narrower sense, that of the latter kind is a discrete form or a form of combination."

On the concepts of the identity and difference of posited acts of thought by mere combination and separation, Grassmann builds his magnificent structure of a theory of forms in general, of which arithmetic, geometry, algebra, mechanics, phoronomics, and logic appear to be applications only of special kinds. He is in need of no axioms whatever. The only postulates are such as these: Arithmetic is a system of first degree; plane geometry is a system of second degree; and space is a system of third degree. Plane geometry has two dimensions, and, therefore, if we have one point fixed, two magnitudes are required for the determination of any other point. Space has three dimensions, so that taking a fixed point three magnitudes are necessary for the determining of any other point. Colors, it appears, are another system of third degree; they can be reduced to three primary colors: red, orange, and blue. Accordingly three magnitudes are required for determining any kind of tint. A distinguished scientist has invented a method of graphic representation of colors by triangles.

We cannot have any intuitive conception of a space having four dimensions. Nevertheless, pure mathematics, being independent of dimensions, applies just as much to systems of four and more degrees as to the actual space of three dimensions. The regularity of every system is fixed a priori by the elements posited for that system. The elements, positing themselves or being posited by us according to the rigid rule of strict consistency, will necessarily form a regular and orderly arranged system. We can therefore state with absolute precision all the formal laws by which bodies of four or five dimensions, if they existed, would be governed.*

The chief difference between the numbers of arithmetic, geometrical planes, mathematical space,

---

* As an example we may use the instance, that the product of two magnitudes in a system of second degree can be algebraically expressed by

$$(a + b)^2 = a^2 + 2ab + b^2,$$

in a system of third degree, by

$$(a + b)^3 = a^3 + 3a^2b + 3ab^2 + b^3$$

in a system of fourth degree, by

$$(a + b)^4 = a^4 + 4a^3b + 6a^2b^2 + 4ab^3 + b^4.$$

Accordingly, a cube or any parallelopipedon which is the product of two magnitudes consists of eight tri-dimensional parts. This fact cannot only be proven a priori by mathematical or algebraical demonstration of purely formal thought, it can be ascertained by experience also. A cube that is cut in all its three dimensions, according to the ratio of a + b, will afford an example, and a body formed by two magnitudes (a + b) in four dimensions, if it were possible, would consist of the following 16 four-dimensional parts:

1. A regular body which in all four directions measures a ($= a^4$).

2. Another regular body which in all four directions measures b ($= b^4$).

3. Four bodies which in three dimensions measure a ($= a^3$), and in one b.

4. Four bodies which in three dimensions measure b ($= b^3$), and in one a.

5) Six bodies which in two dimensions measure a ($= a^2$), and in two b ($= b^2$).

on the one hand, and Grassmann's systems of 1, 2, 3, or *n* dimensions on the other, is, that numbers, planes, and actual space are accepted as given; they are the data of arithmetic, geometry, and mathematics, while the systems constructed by Grassmann's "theory of forms in general" are conceived as products of thought. They are posited by a progress of thought and can be considered as data only if their parts, once posited, are further used as such for combinations among themselves.

It is obvious that the only condition of all kinds of such systems of formal thought is *consistency.* Truth with regard to our knowledge of reality is the agreement of our concepts with the objects represented; but truth in the domain of pure formal thought is the agreement of all posited forms of one and the same system among each other. This consistency is the basis of all law, regularity, and order; and whatever system of forms may be selected, its rules and theorems will be developed by our mind with the same wonderful harmony and precision as can be observed in mathematics, arithmetic, logic, and mechanics. Accordingly, if the world were otherwise than it is, if space had only two, or if it had four dimensions, the laws of the world would be otherwise, but none the less regular than at present—they would be strictly *gesetzmässig, i. e.,* conforming to, and explainable by, law.

Consistency must be considered in the empire of form, as the counterpart of inertia* in the realm of matter. So long as nothing interferes to produce a change,

---

*Inertia in German is sometimes called *Trägheit*, sometimes *Beharrung*. *Trägheit* is the literal translation of inertia; it is a negative term which denotes the non-appearance of new energy, or motion, or activity. *Beharrung* is the better term; it affords a positive expression for "inertia," denoting the unchanged continuance of the energy in existence.

everything will remain as it is. Consistency therefore, the very root of order, from which all order of form in every possible system of forms finds its explanation, is the natural state. Consistency like the law of inertia and the law of identity explains itself. Wherever we meet with it, it need not be accounted for; an explanation becomes necessary only where consistency is lacking. From this consideration it is apparent that to whatever system the form of reality belonged, it could in no case be devoid of order. The world could not be a chaos, but of necessity must be a cosmos.

Grassmann's theory of 'forms in general' throws a new light upon Kant's doctrine of the a priori, since it exhibits a science of pure form in its most generalized abstractness. Thus the a priori has lost the last vestige of mystery and we can easily understand how the cosmical order is due to the formal laws of nature. While Kant's reasoning has been correct in the main, it is apparent that real space is not quite so purely formal as he imagined. A system of form of the third degree can be posited a priori by formal thought; but the fact that real space is such a system of the third degree can be ascertained by experience only.

We have used the word order in the sense of objective regularity which of necessity results from a consistency of form throughout one and the same system. This regularity of forms enables us to think many samenesses by one idea and thus makes an economy of thought possible, which as Ernst Mach declares is the characteristic feature of science. Ernst Mach (who I must suppose has attained to his ideas quite independently of Grassmann, although there is no doubt that both have been strongly influenced by Kant), points out, by a happy instinct as it were, the most practical application of the theory of formal thought in general.

The regularity of form being repeated in the physiological arrangement of the nervous cells and fibres in our brain, produces in man an economy of feeling and thinking which the more it is realized and practiced, gives him the greater power over nature.

v.

CONCLUSION.

ALTHOUGH Kant's Transcendental Idealism cannot be considered as a final solution of the basic problem of philosophy, it nevertheless pursues the right method and has thus actually led us to a solution which, we hope, will in time be recognized as final. In Kant's time, it seemed as if the key to the mysteries of cosmic order should be sought for in nature's manifestations outside of the human mind. Kant, a second Copernicus, reversed the whole situation and pointed out that the key to the problem: "How is nature possible at all?" is to be found in the human mind. And yet the natural sciences, inquiring into the secrets of nature by the observation of natural phenomena, were after all not on a wrong track. Kant and the natural sciences seemed to exclude each other, but they were complementary. Schiller who in so many respects fore-felt and fore-told future events in the prophetic spirit of his poetry, said in one of his Xenions, referring to Transcendental Philosophy and Natural Science:

" Both have to travel their ways, though the one should not know of the other. Each one must wander on straight, and in the end they will meet."

Two truths may at first appear contradictory,

though they are not. Let us not distort the one for the sake of the other, but let each be presented without regard to the other, and let every point of divergency be brought out fully. Theory and practice, formal thought and experience, the thinker and observer, will at last agree better if they boldly take the consequences of their views and combat those of the other. About the relation of transcendental philosophy to natural science in his time, Schiller said:

" Enmity be between both, your alliance would not be in time yet.
Though you may separate now, Truth will be found by your search." ·

There has been enmity enough between philosophy and natural science. Philosophers looked with scorn upon the specialists who confined their labors to narrow circles, and scientists, confident of their positive results, smiled about the phantastic dreams of theoretic speculations. However, in the progress of time, philosophers learned to prize the valuable researches of natural science, and the scientists felt the necessity of a philosophical basis for their investigations and methods of investigation. At present the want of a close contact between philosophy and the sciences is a fact that is freely acknowledged by both, philosophers and scientists.

In Kant's and in Schiller's time an alliance between philosophy and natural science would have been premature. How many futile attempts have been made in the mean time! Fichte, Schelling, Hegel, and Schopenhauer in Germany, the two Mills and Herbert Spencer in England, Auguste Comte in France, have appeared with their systems, partly opposing, partly repeating Kantian ideas in other and original ways of presentation, partly combating his very method, partly popularizing, and at the same time opposing his views.

But none of them (not even Comte*) succeeded in creating a well-established positivism that could dispense with the mystical element altogether, whether it appear as the Transcendent, the Unknowable, or the Supernatural.

We have attempted in these essays on " Form and Formal Thought " to lay the cornerstone of such positivism, which, it is to be hoped, will prove to be the only true Monism, *i. e.*, a philosophy free from contradictions and in accordance with reality, thus offering a basis for a unitary and harmonious conception of the world.

* See foot-note on page 67.

THE OLD AND THE NEW MATHEMATICS.*

In mathematics, just as in all sciences and in religion, we have an orthodoxy sanctioned by the authority
of many centuries. This orthodoxy represents a conception of things, which in the past, to some extent,
has proved sufficient for our needs. It is presented in
the most direct, and for its purpose therefore in the
best method — namely in the shape of dogmatism.
Thus matters are, we are told, and it suffices to know
that they are so.

The representatives of orthodoxy are opposed by a
class of heretics, who claim that humanity would have
progressed more rapidly but for the impediments of
dogmatism. The ideas of dogmatism, they say, are fundamentally erroneous, and must be overturned. Room
must be made for doubt. Humanity, up to the date of
the appearance of heretical views, it is held, has been
erring under the dominance of orthodoxy, and we must
commence to live the life of mankind over again.

These heretics, tearing down and criticizing the old
dogmatism, are by no means useless, or nefarious, or
dangerous men, although they are very often looked
upon as acting the *rôle* of Mephistopheles and although, as a rule, they exhaust their power in more ne-
gations without being able to build anew. Voltaire said:
"If God did not exist, we should invent him." Sim-

* Written in answer to a criticism of Dr. Edward Brooks, of Philadelphia.

ilarly we can say: "If the devil did not exist, we should invent him." "The spirits who deny" play a very important part in the household of nature.

> " Man's aspiration flagging seeks too soon the level,
> Unqualified reposé he learns to crave ;
> Whence, willingly, the comrade him I gave   ′
> Who works, excites, and must create as Devil."

The negative criticism of heresy leads the orthodox conception to a higher plane of development, not by tearing down, but by forcing us to remould it, to elim- inate its errors, and thus to unify its tenets with the other facts of reality.   If we really had to commence to live the life of humanity over again, we would again have to start with the old or a similar dog- matism, until we were sufficiently matured to enlarge our views to a broader conception, in which our former orthodoxy is not so much destroyed as outgrown.

Dr. Brooks represents the orthodox standpoint of mathematics.   He dogmatically believes in the finality of mathematical axioms; he says: "To know how we know the axioms to be true would be equivalent to proving them to be true."   But he does not believe that we can know this *how*.   "There is no 'how,'   he says. * * We just know that they are true and that is the end of it. * * To prove a truth is to establish it by some other truth; but there are no truths back of or before these axiomatic truths which authenticate them.   They are absolutely first truths, underived and self-existent, and as such are cognized by the mind."

This standpoint of orthodox dogmatism in mathe- matics may be called the intuitive method.   In oppo- sition to it John Stuart Mill proposes his heterodox views, which are best characterized as the empiricist method.   Mr. Mill says in his System of Logic (2, V. Sec. 1):

"The points, lines, circles, and squares which any one has in his mind, are (I apprehend) simple copies of the points, lines, circles, and squares which he has known in his experience. The idea of a point I apprehend to be simply our idea of the *minimum visibile*, the smallest portion of surface which we can see. A line as defined by geometers is wholly inconceivable."

If Mr. Mill's empiricism were correct, mathematics would be an experimental science, like chemistry and the other natural sciences. There would be no difference between formal sciences and experimental sciences, and such things as necessity or necessary truths would be illusions. Mr. Mill accepts this consequence and tries to eliminate "necessity." He says:

"This character of necessity, ascribed to the truths of mathematics, and (with some reservations to be hereafter made) the peculiar certainty, attributed to them, is an illusion. * * *

"When, therefore, it is affirmed that the conlusions of geometry are necessary truths, the necessity consists, in reality, only in this, that they correctly follow from the suppositions from which they are deduced. Those suppositions are so far from being necessary that they are not even true; they purposely depart, more or less widely, from the truth. The only sense in which necessity can be ascribed to the conclusions of any scientific investigation, is that of legitimately following from some assumption, which, by the conditions of the inquiry, is not to be questioned."

According to Mr. Mill, our mathematical conceptions "are not even true; they purposely depart, more or less widely, from the truth." They certainly would depart from the truth if mathematics were an experimental science, if mathematical lines were images of material lines, perhaps of lead-pencil lines, if the mathematical point were truly a *minimum visibile*, etc. Mathematical concepts depart from the real diagrams which we draw for the purpose of assisting our mathematical imagination, but they do not, therefore, depart from the truth.

If Mr. Mill's theory were correct, if mathematics were not a creation of pure formal thought, invented for properly comprehending the laws of pure form, if it were based upon the inaccurate, unreal, and, therefore, untrue images of material points, lines, circles, planes, etc., we would have to remodel the whole science of mathematics so as to make our conceptions of points and lines and planes "true." But an experimental mathematics of that kind, it need not be said, would lose all its value, its certainty, and its exactness. Indeed, as a system of purely formal laws, it would be "untrue"; for it would conflict with the principle of mathematical conceptions that limits the field of mathematics to pure forms and excludes from it any kind of material existence.

The basis of mathematics is pure formal thought. The pure form of a thing is the spacial relation of its parts among themselves. The pure form of a leaden ball is its globular shape. Mathematics, accordingly, deals with the laws of spacial relations purely, without taking into consideration anything else. ﹅ All other qualities, especially those relating to matter and force, are rigidly excluded.

Dr. Brooks says: "Some things not only exist but their existence is a necessity. They exist independently of all conditions and are subject to no contingencies." Among these things, time, and space, and axiomatic truths are classed. The paper, he says, "has length, breadth, and thickness; length, breadth, and thickness are possible only in space, therefore space also exists."

Certainly space exists, but it does not exist of itself. It has no absolute existence. It exists as a property of reality, and our conception of space has been abstracted from reality. 'Length, breadth, and thickness,' we propose to say, '*are* space.' If we say with Dr. Brooks, they "are possible only in space," the dualistic error is near at hand, that space is not a mere abstract idea representing the quality of extension abstracted from extended things, but that it is something existing of itself; something which is the condition of extension, which makes it possible that things can have length, breadth, and thickness.

Space being an abstract and not a thing of itself has been supposed by some philosophers to be a non-entity. Descartes says,* that if that which is in a hollow vessel were taken out of it without anything to fill its place, the sides of the vessel, having nothing between them would be in contact. This is erroneous. Space is not a non-entity, but a real property of things. The spacial relation between two sides of a hollow vessel remains the same whether there is or is not any matter between them. If we could succeed in annihilating the whole world, all spacial relation would be destroyed with it. But let there be one atom only, or one given point, where in our imagination we may place ourselves, and we will therewith establish a possibility of motion in all directions, and the possibility of constructing in our imagination other points in different distances or relations: we would have space—not a part of space, but space entire. Space being the possibility of motion, is determined by measurable relations, in which existences or possible existences or points can be arranged. A part of space, alone and absolute, can neither be created nor can it be annihilated; for space being of itself a mere possibility of relations, is always entire. Thus the min-

* Princip. Phil. II. 18.

utest part of a parabola contains the law of the whole parabolic curve into infinity, and so with the slightest part of space the whole of space is determined.

The old orthodox view of mathematics takes its stand on axioms (such as "a straight line is the shortest distance between two points"), which are accepted as self-evident truths. Among the simplest mathematical theorems is one stating that "the corresponding angles of parallels cut by a straight line are equal." Since an exact proof of this theorem was impossible, it has found a place among the axioms, and is in our textbooks usually treated as such.

Some mathematicians, however, did not rest satisfied with this solution of the Gordian Knot in the fashion of Alexander, and attempted to develop a geometry in which the theorem of corresponding angles should not be accepted as an axiom. They succeeded in establishing a new kind of geometry which was different from Euclid's geometry. Two straight lines cannot inclose a space according to Euclid; but in the new geometry, two straightest lines, if sufficiently prolonged, can inclose a space. To distinguish them from Euclidian "straight lines," it has been proposed to call them "straightest lines," both (straight as well as straightest lines) being the shortest possible distance between two points.

This new geometry has been called that of curved space, and further investigations of acute mathematicians[*] showed that there are two kinds of curvature, the positive and the negative. The Euclidian theorems now appeared as special instances of this geometry. They

---

[*] Further details in a popular form will be found in *Helmholtz,* "On the Origin and Significance of Geometrical Axioms," and in *Dr. Victor Schlegel,* "Ueber den sogenannten vier-dimensionalen Raum."

can be considered as constructed in a plane the curvature of which is zero.

We learn from the attempts made in this direction that the mathematical axioms are by no means "absolutely first truths, underived and self-evident." They depend upon the special condition that the space curvature is zero, which (however justified for practical purposes) has been tacitly assumed.

*   *   *

We can generalize the concept space and consider the line as a space of one dimension, the plane as a space of two dimensions, and actual space as a space of three dimensions. It is impossible to form any intuitive conception of a space of four and, still less, of more than four dimensions. Nevertheless, we can abstract from dimensions altogether and conceive of such absolute space as 'Form, pure and simple.' In doing so we can lay down the laws which are equally valid for all kinds of spaces, whether of three, or four, or n dimensions. Algebra, indeed, is an abstraction of that kind, and algebraic laws are equally valid whether their symbols indicate lines, or planes, or solid bodies, or other things, as for instance logical concepts.

The ultimate step which can be taken in this direction is that of establishing a "theory of pure forms," as has been done by Grassmann. Grassmann recognizes no axioms whatever. He builds his "system of pure forms in general" and finds that Euclid's geometry, as well as the actual space of three dimensions, are special cases only of innumerable other possibilities, the laws of which are all contained in his "theory of forms in general." What Euclid called axioms are a few characteristic features which can be derived from the supposition that plane geometry is a system of second degree. Far from being first, or absolute, or independent truths, the axioms depend upon this supposition, and are applicable only for cases where it is avowedly accepted or at least tacitly assumed.

Grassmann no longer stands alone in the position he has taken; he has found followers who more and more realize that he has been the pathfinder of a new and fertile field of mathematical investigation. The ultimate basis of mathematics is no longer the intuition of space but the conception of "abstract form in general." The apriority of the mathematical laws of actual space has to be limited to the extent that we can know by experience only that actual space has three dimensions, and we have learned to consider the world-space as one actual instance among many theoretical possibilities: it is a formal system of third degree.

Actual space, abstracted from reality, is a quality of real things representing their relations, the relations of their parts, and the possible directions of their motion. But actual space, as we can ascertain by experience, is at the same time a system of third degree. As a system of third degree, it is a creation of our mind, it is purely formal thought, to which all the rigidity and universality of formal laws is attached. The sentence "space is a system of third degree," is as little tautological, or begging the question, as that the earth is a spheroid; and it is at the same time just as much a matter of experience. The laws of a system of third degree apply to actual space with the same necessity as the principles of mathematical geography apply to the earth.

*   *   *

Dr. Brooks says: "Some truths are not only true,

but they are necessarily true," and "the mind has the power of knowing that they are necessarily true."

That gunpowder explodes is true; but it is not necessarily true. In damp weather it may not explode; the explosion depends upon certain conditions. But if all the conditions upon which, according to our experience, the result is contingent are fulfilled, we assume that it will explode. It ought to and very likely it will; but must it necessarily explode? Certainly not! There may be one condition which in all former cases was always fulfilled without our knowing it. If this one condition were absent in an eventual experiment the usual result would *not* take place. The results of experimental sciences are never necessary in this rigid sense. Rigid necessity does not depend upon conditions; it is intrinsic and we must be able to verify it as a necessity; we must know why or how it is a necessity, not by intuition, but by proof.

All formal truths are rigid necessities. Propositions, as for instance $2 \times 2 = 4$, and $(a + b)^2 = a^2 + 2\,ab + b^2$, possess intrinsical truth; for they do not depend upon external conditions, and hold good everywhere and for all possible cases.

For the sake of distinction, the truths of purely formal thought are called *correct*, and the truths of a well-ascertained experience *real*. Correct, accordingly, signifies that which is true in a mere formal sense, and real (in this limited sense) signifies that which has a material existence. Mr. Mill, therefore, in the above quoted passage, should have said that the mathematical suppositions are not realities (*viz.*, realities in the limited sense). They are not material existences. But that is no reason for declaring that they depart from the truth. If they are but correct, they are true;

they are true so far as their form is concerned. By correctness we cannot gain substantial knowledge of things, but the correctness of our formal thought alone can afford that necessity, by means of which any kind of truth is established. Without the assistance of arith- metic, mathematics, mechanics, and logic, scientific knowledge cannot be obtained.

The assumption of Dr. Brooks that there are neces- sary truths, of which the mind has the power of know- ing by intuition that they are necessarily true, would lead us back to the conception of "innate ideas." If we are not bound to explain why or how certain ideas are true, there is no means of discriminating between inveterate or inherited errors, and genuine truths.

The existence of the material universe is by no means necessary; nor is it necessary that actual space has three dimensions. We can imagine that we did not exist and that the whole world did not exist; we can imagine that a world existed, the space of which would possess two dimensions. But we cannot think it possible that 2 x 2 = 5; and we can positively under- stand why the laws of form in general must hold good under all conditions and in all possible worlds. If they were never realized in actual existences, they would nevertheless remain what they are—correct.

* * *

In the province of mathematics we move in an at- mosphere of abstract thought. The simplest mathe- matical conceptions are by no means so absolutely simple as they appear; they are simple only in com- parison with other mathematical ideas, definitions of, and theorems about, complex figures. A bright little boy of six years may have very clear conceptions as to dogs, horses, and even engines or other concrete

things, but there is little probability of his understanding the meaning of a mathematical point. That simple
idea is too complex for his immature comprehension.
Dr. Brooks says:

"A derivation of one truth from one or more other truths is
called reasoning. * * * All reasoning can be traced back to truths
which cannot be derived from other truths, and hence are not the
result of reasoning."

According to our view the basic conceptions of
mathematics and the axioms so-called, *are* the result
of reasoning. They are not first truths from which
we start quite from the beginning; they are not self-
evident in the sense that there are no truths back of
or before them; but we acquire them after a long exercise in mental work only. They are based upon a
well-directed and disciplined discrimination. This discrimination between form and matter, simple though
it appears to us now, is most subtle, and its importance is invaluable. It enables us to construct systems
of, and to evolve the laws pertaining to, formal thought.
This discrimination between form und matter is, therefore, the commencement of a higher development; it
makes scientific thought possible.

The correctness of formal knowledge was formerly
based on axioms which had to be taken on faith.
But as long as the certainty of axioms is based upon
intuition, mathematics (and all other formal sciences)
must appear to hover in the air and have no connection with the solid facts of reality. Mathematicians,
it is true, rarely were inclined to foster mystic views
(Cabalistic and Neoplatonic mathematicians are exceptions), and Dr. Brooks also repudiates any kind
of mysticism. Nevertheless as long as a science is
ultimately based on intuition, there is room for any

degree of mysticism. Grassmann's broader conception of mathematics has made all mysticism impossible. He has taught us to dive down to the bottom
of the problems, where we can understand the origin
and whole growth of mathematics and where they are
seen to be in connection with the other facts of reality.

*   *   *

For our present purpose we are satisfied with having pointed out the connection which obtains between
mathematics and the other facts of reality; but we
may add for those interested in the philosophy of mathematics, that from Grassmann's standpoint the connection, also, that exists between the different mathematical theorems and solutions is more readily understood. Hamilton's quaternions and the significance
of imaginary quantities have been anticipated by
Grassmann and appear in their connection with his
system in a new light. Grassmann's method allows a
survey of the whole field and thus gives to the student that easy freedom which a traveler feels who
constantly keeps in sight the point towards which he
is journeying, as well as the road on which he approaches it.

Grassmann says*:

"Since both mathematics and philosophy are sciences in the
strictest sense of the term, the methods employed in each must
accordingly have something in common, which gives them their
peculiar scientific character. Now, we give a scientfic character
to a method of treatment when the student, on the one hand, is
of necessity led by it to the recognition of every single truth, and
on the other hand is placed in a position wherefrom he is enabled,
at every point in the development, to survey the course of further
progress.

*Grassmann, "Die lineale Ausdehnungslehre, ein neuer Zweig der Mathe-
matik," Introduction, page xxxi.

" The indispensableness of the first requirement, *viz.*, *scientific rigidity*, every one will admit. As to the second, the same remains a point that is not as yet sufficiently recognized by the majority of mathematicians. Demonstrations are frequently met with, where, unless the theorems were stated above them, one could never originally know what they were going to lead to; here, after one has followed every step, blindly and at haphazard, and ere one is aware of it, he at last suddenly arrives at the truth to be proven. A demonstration of this sort, perhaps, leaves nothing more to be desired in point of rigidity. But scientific it certainly is not. The second requisite is lacking — namely, *the power of survey.* A person, therefore, that goes through such a demonstration, does not attain to an untrammelled cognizance of the truth, but he remains—unless he afterwards, himself, acquires that survey—in entire dependence upon the particular method by which the truth was reached. And this feeling of constraint which is at any rate present during the act of reception, is very oppressive for him who is wont to think independently and unimpededly and who is accustomed to make his own by active self-effort all that he receives. If, however, at every point in the development, the student is put in a position to see at what he is aiming, he remains master of his material, he is no longer bound to the particular form of presentation, and his assimilation of what he attains becomes actual reproduction."

74

Metaphysics: The Use and Meaning of the Word.

KANT calls every transcendental (or a priori) judgment 'metaphysical,' and the science of pure (or a priori) conceptions 'metaphysics.' Metaphysical notions, accordingly, are such as are true even if not confirmed by practical experiment, such as can not be refuted by experience. They are rigidly necessary and universal. Kant might have called metaphysics the mathematical or formal aspect of things.

The metaphysics of natural sciences is what Kant calls "pure natural science" (*Reine Naturwissenschaft*), and the law of Causation is one of the most important truths of pure natural science.

The doctrine of the 'Conservation of Matter and Energy,' although it has been discovered with the assistance of experience, can be proved in its full scope by pure reason alone. And therefore it would be, according to Kant's terminology, a metaphysical cognition.

Other philosophers have used the word metaphysics in a different sense. Perhaps misguided by a wrong etymology or at any rate under the influence of the literal meaning of the word, they attached to the term the idea of a science that investigates into that which lies behind nature. This unknown something was considered as the source and origin of natural phenomena. Schopenhauer says:

" By metaphysics I understand every pretended cognition which goes beyond experience and therefore beyond nature or the given appearance of things in order to give information about that upon which nature somehow is dependent, popularly expressed what is behind nature and makes nature possible." (Translated from "*Welt als Wille und Vorstellung,*" Vol. II. 2d ed. p. 180.)

The term metaphysics has become popular in the sense conceived by Schopenhauer. No wonder that Comte, from the standpoint of positive philosophy, denounced metaphysics as radically erroneous. Before he was acquainted with Kant's works, he considered him as the representative metaphysical philosopher. Later on when he had read one of Kant's writings, he acknowledged in a letter to a friend,* that at every point Kant showed the spirit of positivism. A republication of the letter is found in the preface to Max Müller's translation of Kant's "Critique of Pure Reason."

The name metaphysics is due to a misunderstanding. Aristotle teaches that natural science ($\phi \nu \sigma \iota \kappa \grave{\eta} \ \phi \iota \lambda o \sigma o \phi \acute{\iota} a$) must be treated according to ceartain principles ($\dot{a} \rho \chi a \acute{\iota}$);

* ' J'ai lu et relu avec un plaisir infini le petit traité de Kant (*Ideen zu einer allgemeinen Geschichte in weltbürgerlicher Absicht, 1784*): il est prodigieux pour l'époque, et même, si je l'avais connu six ou sept ans plus tôt, il m'aurait épargné de la peine. Je suis charmé que vous l'ayez traduit, il peut très-efficacement contribuer a préparer les esprits à la philosophie positive. La conception générale ou moins la méthode y est encore métaphysique, mais les détails montrent à chaque instant l'esprit positif. J'avais toujours regardé Kant non-seulement comme une très-forte tête, mais comme le métaphysicien le plus rapproché de la philosophie positive.... Pour moi je me trouve jusqu'à present, après cette lecture, d'autre valeur, que celle d'avoir systématisé et arrêté la conception ebauché par Kant à mon insu, ce que je dois surtout à l'éducation scientifique; et même le pas le plus positif et le plus distinct que j'ai fait après lui, me semble seulement d'avoir découvert la loi du passage des idées humaines par les trois états théologique, métaphysique, et scientifique, loi qui me semble être la base du travail dont Kant a conseillé l'exécution. Je rends grâce aujourd'hui à mon défaut d'érudition; car si mon travail, tel qu'il est maintenant, avait été précédé chez moi par l'étude du traité de Kant, il aurait à mes propres yeux beaucoup perdu de sa valeur. Auguste Comte par E. Littré. Paris, 1864, p. 154. Lettre de Comte à M. d'Eichthal, 10 Déc. 1824.'

We must add, that to our conception Comte was more metaphysical even than Kant, for he still believed in the Unknowability of what he called " first and final causes," and considered only " the middle between them " accessible to cognition. His conception of positivism was to limit science to the positively knowable; but he did not succeed in entirely freeing his philosophy from mysticism—which after all is the primary object of all philosophy.

therefore it is no independent science. He calls the science of these principles the first, and natural science the second philosophy* (πρώτη καὶ δευτέρα φιλοσοφία). The first science, the philosophy of principles, is treated in a book which in the collection of Aristotelean works had been placed immediately after the books on physics, and some ingenious commentator or copyist, unable to find a proper title, inscribed the essays on the first science τὰ μετὰ τὰ φυσικά (sc. βίβλια) "The books after the physical ones." From the words μετά (after, behind), and φυσικά (physical) the term metaphysics has been coined, which gave rise to so many errors and seemed so appropriate and expressive to dualistic philosophers.†

Metaphysics, as employed by Kant, is the most important and most valuable study we have. It is the theoretical basis for all scientific knowledge. Metaphysics, as a science that should give us information about the origin of existence at large, is generally called ontology, or the science of absolute being. Metaphysics, in the sense of ontology, has become, since Kant, untenable ground; and, therefore, Kant has been commended for having given the *coup de grace* to metaphysics.

Goethe and Schiller did not misconstrue the tendency of Kant's criticism, when they declared in one of their Xenions:

> " Since Metaphysics of late without heirs to its fathers is gathered,
>   Here at the auctioneer's are ' things of themselves ' to be sold."

---

* εἰ μὲν οὖν μή ἐστί τις ἑτέρα οὐσία παρὰ τὰς φύσει συνεστηκυίας, ἡ φυσικὴ ἂν εἴη πρώτη ἐπιστήμη· εἰ δ'ἐστι τις οὐσία ἀκίνητος, αὕτη προτέρα καὶ φιλοσοφία πρώτη.—Arist. Metaph. v. 1.

† Titulum vulgatum τὰ μετὰ τὰ φυσικά non ab ipso esse Aristotele his libris inscriptum, adeo est verisimile ut pro certo haberi possit. *Bonitz,* ad Arist. Metaph., p. 3.

Metaphysics, in the sense of first principles, would be a clarification of our most general ideas, which, like logical theorems, are most obvious truths. Schiller occasionally jests about the subject, saying in one place:

> " Metaphysicians know, I'm told,
> That what is hot cannot be cold;
> Light is not dark, they'd bet,
> And dry things are not wet."

The more a statement is generalized, the less positive knowledge will it contain. The most general laws, which imply absolute universality, are merely formal and do not contain any positive knowledge, however important they may be for the purpose of orientation, so as to enable us to locate and map out our different cognitions according to a systematic method; and those philosophers who assume an air of profound wisdom when speaking about metaphysics are satirized by Schiller in the following lines:

> " How deep the world beneath me lies;
> My craft the loftiest of all
> Lifts me so high, so near the skies
> I scarce discern the people crawl."

> Thus shouts Tom Roofer from his spire,
> Thus in his study speaks with weight
> Metaphysicus, the learned sire,
> That little man, so high, so great.

> That spire, my friend, proud and profound.
> Of what is 't built; and on what ground?
> How came you up? What more is 't worth,
> Than to look down upon the earth?

Mephistopheles, in Goethe's Faust, treats the subject in a well-known passage with great sarcasm. He satirizes those metaphysicians who are pleased to veil their language in mystical and contradictory expressions, which either contain trite truisms in the shape of philosophical conundrums, or must be classed with hallucinations and other pathological phenomena of a diseased brain. Mephistopheles says:

Metaphysics, in the sense conceived by Schopenhauer, and combated by Comte, is the last remnant of
theological supernaturalism.   It is dualism, pure and
complete, without religious mythology.   The mythological entities have been volatilized in the crucible of
philosophy to vague shadows of a transcendent or
metaphysical something.   This something is supposed
to be " the thing of itself," the ultimate x in all philosophical problems, and the unknowable, eternal reality
behind the knowable transient phenomena.   Metaphysicism of this kind has been and will more and more be
superseded by Positivism.

THE PROBLEM OF CAUSALITY.

CAUSALITY, the law of causation, is the basis of all our experience, and a clear conception of causality is indispensable to correct observation as well as to sound reasoning. In spite of this, the problem of causality has been unbecomingly neglected; the vagueness of terms, the lack of lucidity, and the innumerable errors springing from such uncertainty are astounding. Expressions such as 'first cause,' 'ultimate cause,' 'final cause,' 'remoter cause,' 'general cause,' 'universal cause,' '*causa sui*' are in vogue among thinkers of no inconsiderable repute. In elucidating the problem, we shall first propose a few examples, then our definitions, then some explanations, and finally discuss the erroneous conceptions of causality.

EXAMPLES.

I. A sculptor is modeling in clay; after much pressing, trimming, and finishing, a figure is shaped. The form of the statue is the effect of his work. [Production of a new form of matter.]

II. A key on the piano is touched, the hammer strikes the chords, and a sound is produced. The sound is called the effect. [Production of a new form of energy.]

III. A chemist brings hydrogen and oxygen together. An explosion takes place and water is produced. The water is called a product of the combination, and the form in which hydrogen and oxygen are combined in water is the effect; of which the combination (the act of combining) is the cause. [Creation of a new form of matter, being another substance and exhibiting new properties.]

IV. The trigger of a loaded gun, pointed toward a deer, is pulled. The deer is hit and dies. The pull on the trigger is the cause, and the death of the animal is the effect. [Destruction of form.]

V. During a rainless season water is poured every evening on an almost withered plant. The plant commences to thrive, it grows and sprouts, and after a while it brings forth blossoms. The plant's blossoming is the effect of its repeated irrigation. [An example from the vegetable kingdom.]

VI. A mother loving her child more than her life, observes that a lion of a menagerie is at large in the market-place. All people flee. Her baby is left behind by its nurse and the lion approaches the infant. The mother rushes out of the house and rescues her child in the face of the lion. [An example taken from human life; the story is an historical fact, known under the title of "The Mother of Florence." The cause, in this case, is the motive of the mother; the effect is the rescue of the child. The motive is mostly a very complicated state of mind, which in the present instance can be summarily characterized as a mother's desire to save her child.]

EFFECT.

The effect has not existed before. It has been produced by its causes. What then is the effect?

Matter cannot be created, and energy cannot be

created; the effect, therefore, can only be a *new form* of matter and energy:

I. The clay of the sculptor existed before the statue; the form of the statue alone is new.

II. A sound is a special vibration of air. The air (in instance No. II) is not created nor is the motion of the air created out of nothing. The vibration of the sound is nothing but transmitted energy coming from the muscular action of the finger that struck the key. The effect, accordingly, is a special form of energy agitating the air.

III. The material elements of the water (H_2O) existed before their combination. The water, in so far as its material particles are concerned, has not been produced. The effect of a chemical combination of H_2O can be called water in so far only as water signifies the *form* into which the elements have combined. In common language we make no distinction between water as matter and as a combination of the two elements.

IV. The death of an animal caused by violence or by natural sickness is destruction of form. True, it is a destruction of life, but life is not a material object, not a thing of substance; life in the narrower sense (the individual life of a deer) is the spontaneous activity of a certain body; it is a form of nerve-energy. Life in the broadest sense of the word, meaning force, or spontaneity, or self-motion, with which all matter is endowed, can not be destroyed. It is indestructible, as we know from the law of conservation of energy. But life in the narrower sense is a certain combination of energy in the special form of an animal body. Death is the destruction of this form; while propagation, being growth and transmittance of form, is a continuance of the paternal form of life in offspring.

V. The blossom of a plant is not the effect of its irrigation. The matter of the blossom, the elementary particles of which the blossom consists, have existed before as water, air, and parts of the soil. And the vegetative energy stored in its cells has also existed in the shape of sunbeams or otherwise. The effect produced is this special form, in which by assimilation and transformation the organs of the plant have combined energy and matter as a blossom.

Definition. Accordingly effect is a new state of things: a new arrangement; a new form produced through some alteration of circumstances.

CAUSE.

The previous state of things, which existed before any effect was produced, cannot have been at rest. If it had been at rest, no effect would have been possible. The previous state of things must have been in motion. Without motion no causation. Motion is an alteration of place. When properly combined, the atoms of oxygen and hydrogen will shape themselves into new configurations. The cause is a motion; it is their properly meeting each other. The atoms being of a certain size and shape, and having special powers of attraction, so that they fit to one another, appear in the new form of water.

A chemist who makes the experiment has, as a matter of course, to observe all the conditions under which the process takes places.

A gardener who waters a plant must at the same time take care that the plant receives sufficient sunlight, that it stands in good soil, and is protected from injurious insects. These facts taken altogether, are called the circumstances. Circumstances in so far as they are indispensable to the realization of an effect, are called conditions

Definition. Cause (being the factor that produces the effect or the new state of things) is a motion. It is an alteration in a certain state of things whereby a further alteration, a re-arrangement or a new combination, becomes necessary.

EXPLANATIONS.

1. *Causes and Conditions.* It is obvious that if in a certain state of affairs the effect is produced by several, perhaps simultaneous, movements, we may arbitrarily call one of them the cause and the other ones its conditions, or we may call all of them together the causes. So for instance, the sunbeams (not as things, but as a motion, as ether-vibrations) may be called the cause of blossoming just as well as the watering; or we may designate both as the common causes.

2. Cause and effect are two states, the one following the other: The causal state disappears by creating the state of the effect; or in other words, the cause, vanishing as such, reappears in the effect. The same matter, the same energy are exhibited in a new form or a new combination.

3. The scholastic maxim, *cessante causa cessat effectus,* is accordingly wrong. The cause is always passed, if the effect is produced.

4. Causes and effects form an infinite chain of alterations; every cause is the effect of another cause; and every effect can become the cause of another effect. If a key on the piano is touched, a lever is set in motion which raises a hammer; the hammer strikes

against the chords and sinks back; the chords vibrate according to their length and induce in the air corresponding undulations. The air-waves meet a human ear and transmit their rhythmic motions to the tympanum, thence the disturbance passes through many stations in the aural apparatus and reaches the auditory nerve where it is perceived as sound. In this and in all other chains of causes and effects, any of the succeeding stages may be called the effect of its antecedents and the cause of its consequents.

Accordingly the signification of cause and effect is to a great extent arbitrary and depends much upon the proper tact of the observer. He should select as cause and effect two states which somehow correspond to one another in importance for a special purpose. How far the intermediate links can be neglected, depends upon circumstances.

5. Our example No. III (the generation of water) is often used as an instance to prove the transcendence (or unknowability) of the law of causation. However, there is no room for mysticism if we take into consideration that the product is a new molecular form of its constituent elements. By molecular form of water, we understand the combination of H_2 with O in that special form in which it appears as water.

Suppose we have a rectangle of 5 x 3, and two equilateral triangles, the bases of which are 5 and the sides 3. Combine the two bases of the triangles with the longer sides of the rectangle and we will have a hexagon all whose sides are 3. The rectangle, as such, has disappeared, and the triangles, as such, have disappeared also. A new form is created, a hexagon, which has lost the properties of its component figures and possesses properties that were not exhibited in the same. The longer sides of 5 which existed in the triangles as well as in the rectangle are as such altogether lost in the hexagon. The hexagon is equilateral and has six obtuse angles, while the triangles have two acute, the rectangle four right angles, and neither the triangles nor the rectangle are equilateral.

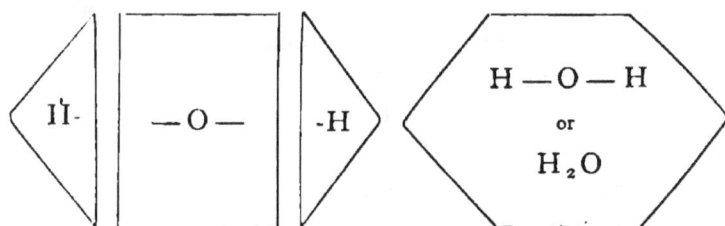

Some imagine that the properties of a combination must have before existed in a latent form; but in our geometrical instance this is evidently impossible. The hexagon is an entirely new form, which has neither existed in the one nor the other of its components. If such is the case in this extremely simple instance, how much the more is it true of the highly complicated combinations and changes of form in reality, which by the smallness of atoms are not directly observable, and can often only be guessed or traced with greatest difficulty!

It is a fact which is overlooked by great thinkers that by combination or change of form things can be created which never existed before in that form, and the qualities of which can neither as latent nor as apparent properties be traced in their constituents.

6. Materialism overlooks the importance of form. While justly opposing the wrong conception of any immaterial existence, materialism goes too far when it considers matter as the only aspect of phenomena, thus making it the sole principle of explanation. Mr.

Spencer tries to reduce everything to matter and motion, and Professor Louis Büchner similarly proposes his philosophy of *Kraft und Stoff*. In this way they fail to see that evolution, progress, the occurrences of inorganic nature as well as the highest aspirations of man, can only be explained from the fact that new combinations or new forms are actually new creations.

It is undeniable that immaterial realities can not exist. The thing exists by its being material; and its reality is manifested by its being a combination of energies; it is a *Kräfte-Complex*. But the thing exists *as such*, because it has a certain form. Destroy the form and the thing as such ceases to exist and changes into something else.

Diamond, graphite, pure coal, and soot, so far as their material constituents are concerned, are the same; all being carbon. And yet they are radically different things, with different properties. Diamond is as white and clear as water and as translucent as air. It is the hardest substance known in nature. Coal, graphite, and soot are of the deepest black, and are soft enough to leave dark, lead-colored traces on paper. Diamond is rare and valuable, while the other formations of carbon abound in nature. The difference of these simple substances is exclusively one of form.

Combinations of the same chemical composition, with different properties, are called isomeric. For instance, the formula $C_2 H_4 O_2$ represents acetic acid as well as methyl ether of formic acid, the former being an acid the latter a neutral substance. The boiling point of acetic acid is almost 90° higher than that of the methyl ether of formic acid, and with same substances the one forms other combinations than the other. Grape sugar, being $C_6 H_{12} O_6$, consists of the same elements in the same proportion also. Quite different from the other two substances, it is sweet, crystalline, capable of fermenting, and neutral to litmus paper. It is neither an acid, a base, nor a salt.

Graphic formulas * have been invented in order to give a visible expression to such differences.

Consequently a thing, a body, a substance, is not only the sum total of its material elements, it is *the form* of its material elements. Materialism is right in so far only as it maintains that things exist at all because they are material; but it must be remembered that they exist *as such* because they have a certain form. Form, so to say, is the soul of things.

The same is true of man. Man is not only an aggregate of matter and energy; he is an aggregate of matter and energy *in a special form*. And it is the form which makes him a man. Prof. Büchner says: †

"The greatest of all poets who has ever lived and whose masterpieces are immortal, because he stood upon this ground of truth and reality, *Shakespeare*, was already a Materialist in his innermost convictions, and with his prophetic eye pursued the

---

* The elements differ in atom-fixing power. An atom of hydrogen, being able to attach to one atom of any other substance, is called a monad, which is expressed by H'; an atom of oxygen is a dyad, O''; nitrogen a triad, N'''; carbon a tetrad, C'''' or C^{iv}. The graphic formula for water is: H—O—H.

Propionic acid, Methyl acetate, and Ethyl formate (all three being $C_3 H_6 O_2$) are, as their names suggest, entirely different substances. They have been expressed by graphic formulas in the following way.

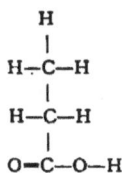

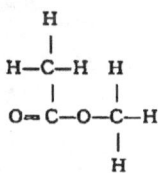

PROPIONIC ACID.   METHYL ACETATE.   ETHYL FORMATE.

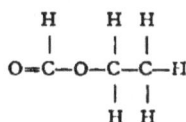

```
      H                      H                 H      H  H
      |                      |                 |      |  |
   H—C—H                  H—C—H  H          O=C—O—C—C—H
      |                      |    |                   |  |
   H—C—H                  O=C—O—C—H              H  H
      |                         |
   O—C—O—H                      H
```

† "Materialism, Its History and Its Influence upon Society." New York. The Truth Seeker Co.

eternal wanderings of matter as the last and primitive cause of everything that exists, through the same pathways, upon which modern science has traced it with mathematical certaintv, when he says (Hamlet, v. 1):

> ' Imperious Cæsar, dead and turned to clay,
> Might stop a hole to keep the wind away;
> Oh! that the earth that kept the world in awe,
> Should patch a wall to expel the winter's flaw!' "

In the bible God says to man: " Dust thou art and unto dust shalt thou return." So, God must have been " already a materialist in his innermost convictions." But this biblical utterance is only one side of the truth, it is the one-sided truth propounded by materialism. The other side of the truth is, that man as such is form; and form is changeable; it can be evolved, and this evolution of form is the purpose of our life, the ideal of our aspirations and the basis of ethics.*

WRONG CONCEPTIONS OF CAUSALITY.

1. Cause is an alteration in a state of things and effect is a new arrangement of things. But cause and effect are never objects or things. A thing by its motion or a person by his labor may produce an effect; but the thing itself or the person is never a cause, nor is the thing produced an effect. A sculptor may carve a statue; the sculptor is not the cause, and the statue as a thing is not the effect. The sculptor's labor is the cause; and the effect is the special *form* of the wood, clay, stone, or bronze, *i. e.*, the statue without reference to its material.

2. God has been called 'first cause.' First causes are of mere relative existence. A first cause is the starting-point in a series of some longer chain of causes and effects. The first cause in our second example is the touching of the key; all the effects of this cause are

later causes in the series. According to the nebular hypothesis of Kant the first cause in the formation of our planetary system must have been an unequal distribution of matter. This state of things happened many billions of years ago, and has passed away, as any cause must disappear when its effect has resulted.

'Ultimate cause' is a synonym of 'first cause.' The first term becomes the ultimate one if we count backwards. The expression 'ultimate cause' is even more unfortunate than first cause.

3. Hume speaks of 'general causes,' meaning thereby natural laws. The Germans distinguish between *Grund* and *Ursache*. *Ursache* is what we have defined as cause; *Grund* is the law by which we explain *why* the cause acts. *Grund* is the *raison d'être*, the reason, the principle, the law according to which things change or move, and according to which men act. For instance, gravitation is not the cause that a stone falls to the ground. The cause may be that my fingers let it go. Gravitation is the *ráison d'être* of a stone's fall in this particular instance as well as in any other case. A cause is a single event, a single fact, a certain motion or alteration. The *raison d'être* of gravitation, however, is a general law and a principle of explanation.

Those who call God the first cause really mean to call God the ultimate ground of the world; they intend to represent him as the most comprehensive principle of existence; as the ultimate generalization of all laws.

4. The scholastic dictum, *cessante causa cessat effectus*, which is quoted above as wrong, refers to this *raison*

---

*Compare Mr. E. C. Hegeler's essay, "The Basis of Ethics," in No. 1 of the OPEN COURT, and the editor's pamphlet, "Monism and Meliorism," V., §5-9.

d'être. It should read, *cessante ratione cessat causatio,* *i. e.*, if the ground or reason, the rationale, ceases to be valid, the cause cannot take effect. For instance, love of freedom was the *raison d'être* of Greek industry, progress, and civilization. As long as this love of freedom prevailed, Greece was free, pros- perous, advancing, and civilized. As soon as this love of freedom yielded to indifference, avarice, and other vices, Greece began to decline. It was a ground but not a cause — it was a continuous principle which manifested itself in many single cases. So the law of gravitation is no cause, but a law recognized in many instances and regulating the causation of gravi- tating objects.

5. The *causa sui* of Spinoza is one of the worst self-contradictions in existence, designating "a cause which is the cause of itself." Spinoza apparently means *ratio sui*, a reason or principle which explains itself; a ground which has its ground in itself, meaning a self-evident truth that for verification does not depend upon some other evidence. Spinoza confounds this *ratio sui* with the idea of an absolute existence; *i. e.*, an existence which contains in itself the ground or *raison d' être* of its existence. On this logical error rests the whole structure of his grand and noble phi- losophy.

6. 'Final cause' is a most unfortunate expression for purpose. The schoolmen distinguished 'effective causes' and 'final causes.' It is obvious that all causes are effective. If a certain cause is the will of a man, the idea which guides him is an indispensable condi- tion. This idea is the end to be attained. If such causes are to be called 'final causes,' we must bear in mind that these 'final causes' are just as much effective

causes as any others. There is no essential difference. Both result into their effects with the same
necessity.

Final cause being an inappropriate synonym of
purpose, has only sense when it is used in reference to
a will. We cannot speak of the final cause of cereals
as being serviceable food for man. There is no final
cause in nature outside of the province of volition.

7. *Causality immanent. The world no chaos, but a
cosmos.* Those who use the word 'final cause' in a more
general sense, imagine that a divine providence has
arranged the order of things according to some plan
or design. They consider the universe by itself as
chaotic, and believe that God imposed law and order
upon it from the outside.

Materialism, denying altogether the existence of
final causes and design in nature, falls into the same
error as its enemy, dualistic superstition. Materialism
also considers the universe as originally chaotic, and
explains the order of the world as the fortuitous outcome of haphazard, which if once happily arranged
has necessarily more stability and more chance. to
continue so than other, chaotic formations. This view
disagrees with facts. The relatively chaotic combinations of lower natural manifestations are more stable
than the higher evolved forms of life, the highest forms
being least stable.

Monism teaches that the order of the universe is
not transcendent; it is not imposed upon nature from
the outside; the order of the world in its mechanical
regularity is immanent. The world is no chaos, it is
a cosmos, and if God is to be called the order of the
universe, monism teaches that God is immanent; God
and the universe are one.

MATTER, MOTION, AND FORM.

In all causative processes we must distinguish three things, Matter, Motion, and Form; and indeed the comprehension of a phenomenon is not complete until we know in what *form matter moves*.

Matter, motion, and form are three abstractions. None of them exists of itself, and no natural phenomenon can be without any one of these three things. The form of existence is called space, and experience teaches us that it is tri-dimensional. All the single forms of reality which are found to exist bodily, therefore, depend upon the laws of a formal system of third degree. A knowledge of these formal laws was for this reason, in ancient Greece, considered as the basis of science and received the name which it still bears, "Mathematics" (from μανθάνειν, to learn, μάθημα, knowledge, μαθηματικός, pertaining to knowledge).

Matter is that which affects our senses. It manifests its existence by certain motions and by filling space. Apart from space and without the capacity of motion matter cannot even be conceived. The most general term by which matter is characterized is mass. Mass denotes the quantity of matter merely, without considering its weight or volume, which vary according to circumstances.

Motion is change of place. But no real motion is possible unless some material particle is moving. Every motion is an alteration of the disposition of matter: it is an alteration of form. Space being the form of reality, all motions depend upon mathematics or laws of space. The science of motion, based on mathematics, is called mechanics.

Motion can be stored up as it were. A pressure with an equal counter-pressure, a stress, is in a state of rest and yet this state of rest contains the possibility of motion, if through some disturbance, acting as a cause, a part of the whole force of these two pressures is set free. Force and energy are concepts which have been framed to account for the innumerable forms of motion and to explain how one form of motion originates, while another disappears. Under certain circumstances apparent rest seems to produce motion; but in reality potential energy is set free; stress or stored up motion is transformed into actual motion.

Monistic tendencies in the domain of philosophy can with a certain consistency result in three different views. One considers Matter as the universal principle from which all phenomena must be explained; the other selects Motion, and the third Form for the same purpose. The first has been called Materialism, the second may fitly be named Dynamism, or Kineticism, and the third appears as Spiritualism or Idealism. All three views lose sight of the fact that matter, motion, and form are mere abstractions and that none of them exists or can exist of itself; they are only three aspects of reality. Reality, being one indivisible whole, possesses properties for which matter, motion, and form are general terms.

Dynamism, in its purest form, has never become prominent. Materialism generally appears combined with Dynamism. Mr. Spencer attempts to explain

everything by Matter and Motion, and Professor
Büchner similarly reduces all to Matter and Force.
Idealists, on the òther hand, look upon form as the
matrix of all existence. Plato attributes to pure form
a higher kind of reality than exists in the province of
material bodies. To him the ideas or pure forms of
things are eternal, while their material realizations
possess a transient sham-existence. They are mere
appearances of phenomenal, not of real, being.

Plato's doctrine of idealism appears to be loftier
than the materialistic conceptions of the world, because an appreciation of form is the basis for comprehending those phases of the world which must be
prized most highly. The cosmic order of the world
must be understood through the laws of form. Mind
is a special form of life. Volition and human action
are special forms of motion, and so are all manifestations of the life of organisms. The rules of the beautiful in the empire of art, the maxims of goodness in
ethics, the laws of truth in science, find their ultimate
foundation in form; and what are ideals if not higher
forms to be realized? Form is, as it were, the spirituality of the world and a neglect of the importance of
form deprives man of all that makes life worth living.

The tendency of our age is materialistic, and materialism has established a most important truth by
insisting upon the fact that there is no reality but in
material existence. But matter, although a most essential feature of reality, is not the whole of it. Man's
personality is not his material being; he is not the sum
total of the atoms of which he consists. Man's personality, his mind, his intelligence, his character, is
the special form in which the atoms have taken shape.
Break this form and his personality is destroyed. Pre-

serve this form, or build it again, and his personality is preserved.

Form admits of change.   It can degenerate and it can even be destroyed, but it can be improved also. Form and the changeability of form, are the conditions of evolution.   It is the possibility of a constant progress resulting therefrom, which gives to life its ethical value.

UNKNOWABILITY AND CAUSATION.*

Mr. Salter says: "The law of causation is perfectly intelligible * * * it is the cause that may be transcendent or unknowable."

In no one of our examples can the causes be transcendent or unknowable. Every cause is a motion or change of place, and although there are many phenomena so complicated that we have not as yet been able to discover their causes, we may be quite sure that the causes exist and that they are motions of some kind, ascertainable and measurable.

The cause, being a motion, is, as a rule, not very difficult to discover. The difficulty commences when we begin to search for reasons. In order to discover the cause of a phenomenon we have to observe the progress of motion, first the touch of the key on the piano, then the rising of the hammer, the vibration of the chord, the vibration of the air, then of the tympanum, then the irritation of the auditory nerve, and the perception of sound. In order to know a cause we must either directly or indirectly experience it. A cause is a fact, an event, an occurrence, that must be stated. Our reason, which is the faculty of comprehending, is called into action when we ask for an explanation of the fact. This explanation is something quite different from the cause of a phenomenon, for it is not a motion, not a single event, not a separate oc-

* In reply to a criticism of Mr. W. M. Salter.

currence but a general law or an abstract rule, a formula that comprehends all possible instances of the same kind.

In former ages skepticism was more powerful and indeed more justifiable than it is to-day. The relativity of knowledge seemed to take all vigor out of science. The human race was recognized to be limited to this earth; how could a man dare to hope ever to know of what the sun and the stars consist! The impossibility of any knowledge of that kind appeared obvious. Man's eye is so constructed that the impressions of light require a certain time and intensity; how can he ever expect to have information about the path of the lightning-flash or about stars whose light is not intense enough to impress the retina? The impossibility of any conception of that kind seemed plainly demonstrable. Man's ear can perceive sounds of certain pitch only; if they are too high or too low they will pass by unnoticed. These imperfections necessarily seemed to preclude man from any knowledge that lay without the range of his sensory organs, which are the basis of all his cognition. And yet, a few simple inventions have admitted us to all these seemingly inaccessible laboratories of nature. It is the very relativity of our knowledge, so often impugned, that allows an indirect, yet most reliable, apprehension, where a direct observation is impossible.

Causes are facts of nature; and although it requires much ingenuity and critical discrimination, it is nevertheless comparatively an easy task to trace them in natural phenomena. Our senses may prove dull in many subtle cases, but instruments for our assistance have been and will be invented. There is nothing to be comprehended in facts, they have simply to be

stated. But the statement of the causes in a phenomenon is the raw material only with which science
works. The causes of a phenomenon being known,
we search for its reason. The reason why the chord
produces a certain sound must be sought in the peculiar
qualities of the chord and its surrounding air; perhaps
also, in the manner in which the chord is struck by
the hammer. The chord possesses elasticity and has
a certain tension. Strings not possessing these qualities will produce other or perhaps no sounds whatever.
If certain qualities are proven to be the conditions of
the effectiveness of the cause, we can easily formulate
this experience into an abstract law which will serve
as an explanation for all instances of the same kind.

The word cause is frequently used to designate
what we have defined as reason or *raison d'être*, although both ideas are two essentially different things.
And the license of language which has sanctioned this
confusion, produces many most perplexing problems.
Now, considering that causes are comparatively easy
to ascertain, while most reasons, even of the simplest
phenomena, can be found only with great difficulty, it
seems probable that Mr. Salter means "reason" not
"cause," when he says: "It is the cause that may be
transcendent." The reasons of innumerable phenomena of nature are still unknown and are supposed to
be unknowable by minds of mystic disposition. But
their being unknown by no means justifies us in considering them as unknowable. The successful solution of so many perplexing problems should encour-
age our scientists to devote their efforts to those problems which now appear hopeless to us.

*   *   *

But the problem whether there is anything unknow·
able in causation lies deeper still. When dualistic
philosophers so confidently speak of the Unknowability of a First Cause, they undoubtedly mean the ultimate *raison d'être* of phenomena, which would be the
most general and therefore universal law, under which
all the other less general laws had to be classified, and
from which they will find their explanation.

If a group of phenomena is classified and formulated into a law, this law represents the reason why
these phenomena occur. But with this the task of
science is not yet exhausted. For our law representing the reason why, demands in its turn an explanation also, and we ask again what is the reason of this
law? When we succeed in finding a reason for this
law, it will be seen to be a more general law which
shows that the first formulated and less general law is
only a special and perhaps at the same time a complicated instance of other, simpler phenomena, with which
we are more familiar.

Let us take, for example, a phenomenon referred
to by Prof. Mach, in his essay, "Transformation and
Adaptation in Scientific Thought."* "Smoke rises
into the air." * * * We formulate a law that "heavy
bodies tend downwards and light ones upwards. It
soon turned out, however, that even smoke had weight,
—and that it was forced upwards only because of the
downward tendency of the air, as wood is forced to the
surface of water because the water exerts the greater
downward pressure." Thus many cases and formulas of quite different phenomena, which at first sight
seemed to be irreconcilable, are comprehended under

* Published in THE OPEN COURT, Nos. 46 and 48.

one more general law. Science went further still.
Newton discovered that the fall of a stone toward the
center of the earth, and the circuit of the moon around
the earth could be classified as two instances of one
and the same law, which has been called by one word
—*gravitation.* Gravitation has so far solved very intricate problems. It has solved them, because we can
think of many phenomena together as being produced
by one and the same quality of matter. To use Professor Kirchhoff's words, we are thereby enabled to
"describe certain phenomena of motion in the most
simple and comprehensive way;" and, as Professor
Mach would express it, we thus "economize our
thought."

Gravitation, which is not yet explained, can just as
little be considered the *omega* of our knowledge in
physics, as the idea of affinity is the *ultimatum* of chemistry. Gravitation demands its explanation also; and
some scientists have ventured on the hypothesis that
both affinity and gravitation are explainable from attraction. Gravitation would be, so to say, the mechanical attraction between two masses, while affinity should
be called molecular attraction. Even if this is true,
we are still very far from seeing the *how* and *why* of
this hypothesis, so as to propose it as a consistent
and obvious theory.*

The further modern science progresses, the more
is the conception of monism realized, which teaches
the unity of truths. All the different truths appear as
so many applications of one and the same law. Now,
suppose that we were in possession of all truths; the
whole universe would be mirrored in our mind, methodically arranged. All the formulas and laws of the
different sciences would be recognized to constitute

* Chemical affinity is now conceived as "transformed heat."

one great system, and one law would be seen to pervade the whole. This supreme law, being the most general, would represent the ultimate *raison d'être* of all the other laws, and it could not, in its turn, be reduced to a still more general law. Accordingly, the modern agnostic says, it is unknowable and it must be transcendent.

Agnosticism is the latest revival of skepticism. The old skepticism declared that we could know nothing: all knowledge is mere opinion, objective truth does not exist. Agnosticism marks a progress in so far as it limits transcendency to the " First Cause "; or, as we would express it, to the ultimate *raison d'être* of the world. There would be no objection to the agnostic idea, if the ultimate *raison d'être* were declared to be the limit of knowledge, the point where our investigation would naturally come to a halt. But then we must know, that the whole of reality, with all its inexhaustible wealth of problems, lies within the bounds of knowability, while beyond that limit is empty nothingness.

Mr. Spencer says:

" For, if the successively deeper interpretations of nature which constitute advancing knowledge are merely successive inclusions of special truths still more general, it obviously follows that the most general truth not admittimg of inclusion in any other, does not admit of interpretation. Manifestly, as the most general cognition at which we arrive cannot be reduced to a more general one, it cannot be understood. Of necessity, therefore, explanation must eventually bring us down to the inexplicable. The deepest truth which we can get at must be unaccountable. Comprehension must become something other than comprehension before the ultimate fact can be comprehended."

Comprehension, it seems, has from the beginning been to Mr. Spencer something different than it is to us. How can it, all of a sudden, change into its contrary? Comprehension is the act of comprehending, or comprising; it is the act of grasping in our mind several things at once, being derived from *com-prehendere*, to grasp together. To understand means the same. *Under*, in the Anglo-Saxon verb *understandan*, has its primary sense of "among, between," as has the German *unter* and the Latin *inter*. *Understandan* means to stand under or in the midst of things, so as to see all their different aspects at once. The Latin *intelligo*, (inter-lego) rests on the same figure of comparison. But the concept and the word 'transcendency' (unknowability) convey the idea that the solution of all problems should ultimately be sought outside of the world, behind or beyond the realm of nature, in another realm which is inaccessible, so that cognition would be obliged to transgress (to transcend) the sphere of knowability in order to get possession of it.

The ultimate *raison d'être*, far from being transcendent, would denote the most immanent quality of things. It would be the most obvious and most simple truth of which all other cases would be more complicated instances, for it would be used to account for all. Certainly, it could not be deduced from a more general statement, and in so far it would be "unaccountable" and "inexplicable." But at the same time there is no doubt that we would need no explanation, and in so far as this could be proven, it would on the other hand be "accountable" and "explicable."

It is a great error to imagine that if we knew this most general law we would be in possession of the key to all the problems of the world. We must not forget that the more a statement is generalized, the emptier the circle of its contents will be of positive information. To know why and how all other instances are special applications of the most general law would be necessary also for their comprehension. Generalization is only one half, discrimination is the other half of comprehension.

Dualistic philosophers have supposed natural phenomena to be mere shadows of the realities behind phenomena.* They looked upon phenomena as visible effects of invisible causes. Cognition, they thought, penetrates through phenomena in order to get a glimpse of the real things. The discovery of natural laws seemed to afford such knowledge of what was considered the real and invisible causes. They appeared as eternal entities behind a transient sham-existence. Taking this view of nature, we shall inevitably come down to mysticism. From this standpoint the truism of the relativity of knowledge would be tantamount to a confession that real knowledge is impossible.

Monism rejects this dualism. The monistic view is positive, and positivism accepts natural phenomena as facts. There is no difference between primary, remoter, and ultimate facts. There is but one kind of facts: such as are real. Real facts, natural phenomena, are at the same time primary and ultimate facts. Knowledge of facts means that they are, as it were, mirrored in our minds. To know a thing means that its image exists in our brain as a feeling nerve-structure, which occasionally can become conscious. Comprehension does not go, and cannot go, beyond facts; but is simply a matter of systematic arrangement. A consideration of this kind, it must have been, that induced Professor Kirchhoff to omit the word "causes"

---

* Plato's simile of the Shadows in the Cavern (Rep. VII) will here be remembered.

in his definition of mechanics.   His work, published
in 1875, commences with these words:

"Mechanics is the science of motion.   Its object we define to
be this: To describe with exhaustive thoroughness and the greatest attainable simplicity the motions that are taking place in nature."   .

In his inaugural address upon entering the Rector-
ate at Heidelberg, in 1865, Prof. Kirchhoff had spoken
of " the causes that condition motion."   The omission
of the word cause, therefore, marks a progress from
metaphysicism (or, at least, the possibility of metaphysicism) to positivism.   All our knowledge is a description of facts, and all our comprehension is economy of thought, through greater simplicity combined
with exhaustiveness.

The law of causation applies to all natural phenomena, but not to nature as a whole; it accounts for
the single things as such; *i. e.*, it explains why they
appear in these special forms.   But the law of causation does not apply to existence *in abstracto*.   Abstract
existence can have no cause; abstract existence is
simply the statement of the self-evident fact that existence exists.

If there is anything transcendent, it is these facts
themselves in their stubborn reality.   All their relations are knowable, all their qualities can be explained,
and their forms accounted for; but their abstract existence, why they are at all, why anything and the
whole world exists, remains, and will remain, what it
always has been—a fact.   If this.absoluteness of facts
is to be called transcendency, we must confess that
transcendency and immanence are two aspects of one
and the same thing, for there is nothing so immanent
in the world as its reality or the fact of its existence.

CAUSES AND NATURAL LAWS.*

Mr. Salter while trying to fit our formula of causation to all possible cases, presents an instance which appears perplexing. "When a stone goes up," he says, "the motion of an arm is a sufficient† cause; but how when the stone comes down? * * * It looks as if there were change without an antecedent motion. The only antecedent motion was that of the rising stone,—and this has exhausted itself."

The problem presented by Mr. Salter must be explained from the Conservation of Energy. The expression that a certain motion exhausts itself is ambiguous and will naturally lead to misconceptions. No motion exhausts itself. It disappears in one special form only to reappear in another form. There are two kinds of energy, potential and kinetic. Kinetic energy (work being performed) is energy of motion, visible or invisible (molecular) motion, heat, electricity, or magnetism. Potential energy is force acting in things at rest —energy of position. A stone of a certain mass lying on the ground, performs no work, but in its weight it represents a certain amount of potential energy. Another stone of the same mass that lies thirty feet above the ground on the roof of a house, repre-

* In reply to a criticism of Mr. W. M. Salter.
† The expression "*sufficient* cause " has been purposely avoided in our discussion on causality. Every cause is a sufficient cause. The mere idea of insufficient causes is productive of confusion. However, reasons may be more or less sufficient.

sents the same amount of potential energy plus the
potential energy equivalent to the kinetic energy ex-
pended in lifting that stone thirty feet. If this stone
is dropped from the roof its additional sum of potential energy is changed during the fall into kinetic
energy. When the stone arrives on the ground it has
lost the kinetic energy of its fall, and by this loss is
created an exact equivalent of heat which, if employed
to raise the stone, could lift it again thirty feet above
the ground.

When a stone is thrown into the air, we transmit
to it kinetic energy. When a stone arrives at the
highest point of its rise, it may be considered as possessing in addition to its weight such potential energy
as is equivalent to the kinetic energy which we have
transmitted to it by the throw. If the stone is not
somehow retained in the air, it will at once change
this potential energy again into kinetic energy; it will
fall down.

Conservation of energy means that the sum total
of all kinetic and potential energy remains the same
in the whole universe. Kinetic energy may be created
from and may disappear into potential energy. There
is no creation in the old sense nor any annihilation,
but only change from one form of energy to another.

In the case presented by Mr. Salter, the cause of
stone's rising to a certain height is the act of throw-
ing; and again, the stone's rising is the cause of its
arrival at a certain height. Its arrival there is the
cause of its falling down. When arrested on the
ground, the stone's downfall is the cause which produces heat. The heat is given off to the surrounding
soil and atmosphere where the further effects become
imperceptible to us; still, they do not cease to exist.

From the beginning of the throw to its subsequent descent the stone never ceases to be in motion, although the velocity of its ascent is constantly decreasing and when it becomes zero, the direction of its motion upwards is changed into a downward direction.

The whole phenomenon is a combination of two forces acting upon the stone: *first*, that of the throw, which is caused by the effort of my hand; and *second*, that of gravity, which is the downward pull towards the earth. (The downward pull is not *caused* by gravity; it *is* gravity. Gravity is a quality that always exists, being in and with things. Therefore we say, "it *is* the downward pull.")

Gravity is continually acting upon the stone; but, inducing in the stone a less momentum at the start than the momentum imparted by the throw, the stone rises. The momentum produced by the force of gravity in the direction of the earth is continually and rapidly increasing and will soon be greater than the momentum produced in the upward direction by the throw, which remains constant. When the stone reaches the highest point of its rise, the momentum induced by gravity has become equal to the momentum imparted by the throw; the stone *seems* to rest for an imperceptible moment before falling; but it is just as much in constant motion as if it were thrown in a curve; *there is no new cause interfering, nor is any new force called into activity.*

Causation is the progress of motion. The progress of motion takes place under certain circumstances (which are to be called conditions, if they are indispensable). The circumstances in this case are the mass of the stone, its distance from the centre of the earth, the mass of the whole earth, the acceleration due to gravity, the resistance of the air, etc. An inquiry into these things and their qualities would afford us the *reason* of the stone's fall; and these reasons, of course, are not motions; they are formulated as natural laws. The circumstances, being certain qualities, are in this case, as in most others, productive of additional motion; potential energy after a change of position is changed into kinetic energy. But without a preceding change of place this would be impossible; there must be a motion (a change of place) of some kind, to *cause* a change.

An avalanche would lie for all eternity on the Alpine ridge if it were not started by some motion. But under certain conditions the flapping wing of a bird might suffice to hurl the whole mass down, thus creating kinetic energy of an enormous amount through an almost imperceptible cause. No phenomenon in nature is without a cause; the cause is always a change of place, a motion of some kind; but the explanation why potential energy is changed into kinetic energy, or why the stone is attracted towards the earth is not the cause but the *raison d'être*, the reason, of a stone's fall. Explanations of the effectiveness of causes under certain conditions are formulated by our scientists into what they call natural laws. Natural laws are abstract conceptions of a certain class of phenomena; they are thoughts which enable us to comprehend all causes of the same kind. Accordingly, gravitation is a law, but not a cause.

Some critical mind may object: "This abstract idea of gravitation which has been formulated by Newton, represents a natural law. Abstract ideas are not real entities, but natural laws are by no means nonentities but realities which exist independent of our thought."

, My answer is: gravitation like all abstract ideas certainly is a non-entity, but in so far only as it does not exist of itself. It is real in so far as it represents a quality which has been abstracted from real things. Abstract gravity as a thing in and of itself is a non-entity; but things exist that possess weight and their quality of possessing weight is called gravity. This quality is real; it exists in certain things independent of our conception.

Qualities are always present in things; they are co-existent with them and in them. Reasons, *raisons d'être*, or grounds, which from the qualities of things account for their actions or motions under certain circumstances are of a general nature; they apply to all cases of the same kind and serve to explain the effectiveness of causes. However, causes are always trantransient phenomena in single and individual cases.

IS NATURE ALIVE?*

MR. SALTER asks: "Is Monism to conduct us back to Mythology? * * * If *causa sui* is a self-contradictory conception what can be said of 'self-motion' or 'spontaneity.' * * * Can a body move itself? If so, what becomes of the definition of cause as motion? If so, there can be change or movement without any antecedent motion."

I.

THE UNIVERSALITY OF LIFE.

MONISM, it is hoped, will not lead us back to Mythology, but will free us from its trammels by explaining it. Mythology, like other errors, and beliefs in ghosts and supernatural entities, leads a hard life because there is some truth in it. The Indian looks upon nature as alive; the things that he sees and hears about him, the rustling leaves of the trees, the babbling brook, the passing cloud, and the silently towering rock, all are supposed to possess life like himself. Is he not a part of nature and should not the rest of nature be similar to him? What is the origin of life, if nature is dead?

Science, no doubt, has put an end to anthropomorphic conceptions. We no longer think that thunder is the work of a thunderer, and that the wind is a restless spirit-hunter who chases the clouds. But the

* In reply to a criticism of Mr. W. M. Salter.

conneçtion between man and nature has by no means
been severed. It has rather become more intimate
than it ever was conceived to be by our ancestors.
The evolution theory has proved the kinship between
man and animals, and later researches concerning the
origin of life arrive at the result that life has no origin:
it must be eternal. The barrier between living organisms and inorganic nature is broken down, and life is
recognized as a fundamental property of matter.

The theory of the immanence of life in nature, as
we may call it, is the result of purely empirical investigations. *Omne vivum ex ovo* was the essence of the
biological investigations of the seventeenth century.
But since the microscope has introduced us into the
mysteries of protoplasm, our modern biologists have
corrected the sentence into: *No living substance but
from living substance.* There is no life but from life
The hypothesis of *generatio æquivoca,* of a spontaneous
generation of life, of heterogenesis, and of a vivification
of so-called dead matter, as it had been supposed to
take place in putrid substances, are now counted
among the many superstitions of science which are
done with forever.

Our view of life itself has been changed at the
same time. Life had been considered as a substance.
What life-substance and mind-substance might be
like, were even not long ago objects of serious discussions. Even so modern a thinker as Mr. Spencer discusses the subject and arrives at the conclusion, so
characteristic of his agnosticism, that it is a problem
too profound for solution.*

The view of life as a substance yielded to the

* Mr. Spencer sums up his opinion in these words: "In brief, a thing cannot at the same instant be both subject and object of thought; and yet the sub-
tance of the mind must be this before it can be known."

belief in a life-principle (a kind of life energy), a view which is generally called vitalism. Vitalism, however, had also to be abandoned, and the life of organisms is now recognized as a phenomenon of nature which depends on the presence of neither a special life-substance nor a life-principle. The phenomenon of organized life appears, as all other phenomena, if its conditions are present; it disappears, if its conditions are absent, and so far as science now goes, life has never been discovered but as a continuation of, or a development from, prior life.

The new view of the immanence of life in nature makes it necessary to distinguish between life in a broader, and life in a narrower sense. Life in a narrower sense appears in the two organic kingdoms as vegetable life and animal life. The lowest kind of organized life exhibits irritability, or sensitiveness to irritations, growth, *i. e.*, alimentation and the assimilation of food, and propagation, which is a special kind of growth. In the animal kingdom, sensitiveness develops sensation and consciousness. Life in the narrower sense, or organized life, in all its wonderful forms, has been developed by imperceptible degrees from life in the broader sense. Life in the broader and broadest sense will be found to be more and more uniform. The highest branches of organized life, however, admit of an almost infinite variety of form.

From the standpoint of a unitary conception of the universe, there is no doubt that the forms of organized life which exist now on our planet, originated from the forms of inorganic life. There was a state of the earth when animal and plant life was impossible. The problem how organized life originated is not yet solved, but there is no reason to consider the problem beyond the reach of science.

The characteristic feature of life in general is self-motion or spontaneity. The spontaneous action of a man originates in his mind and represents his will. Spontaneity or self-motion, however, being the most general feature of life, will be found not only in the organized forms, but also in that kind of life which we call life in a broader sense.

By self-motion, or spontaneity, we do *not* mean a motion to which there is no prior motion and which thus originates out of itself without a cause, or without another motion. Self-motion is used in contradistinction to a movement by push. Suppose, for instance, that the sun in its progress happens to cross the path of a comet, and, being the greater mass, attracts the lonely wanderer. If the attraction of the comet is due to the nature of the comet and of the sun, it is self-motion or spontaneous motion; but if both bodies are inert (inactive), it may be due merely to the push of ether. In either case, whether the motion is spontaneous, *i. e.*, due to an intrinsic quality, or whether it is transmitted by a pressure from without, it could never originate without a cause. A motion of some kind, a change of position, must have happened. This change of position, in this instance the progress of the sun, is according to our conception the cause of the comet's self-motion.

Spontaneity is a quality inherent in all matter and if spontaneously moving bodies have to be called alive we must acknowledge that nature throughout is alive. In this sense Heraclitus said, πάντα πλήρη θεῶν.*

* Literally: "All things are full of Gods" and the saying has always been taken in the sense that all things are *beseelt*, 'en-soul-d'; all things are alive.

The world-substance is not acted upon by pressure, but it acts spontaneously and of itself. Our scientists have attempted in vain to explain the origin of life from dead matter. The truth is that life in a broader sense, *i. e.*, the self-motion of matter, never originated. Life is as eternal as the world, and to search for a beginning of life is as wrong as to search for the origin of matter.

We must well distinguish this kind of life in a broader sense (which is an inherent quality of matter) from the vegetable and animal life of organisms. The former is elementary and eternal; the latter is complex and unstable, because produced by a combination of the former. The life of elementary atoms must be considered as uniform and most simple, that of organisms as manifold and highly complicated.

The word life, however, as commonly understood, is applied to organized life only. Organized life of plants and animals must be recognized as a special form of the universal life, *viz.*, of life in a broader sense. In addition to spontaneity organized life must possess special features which should find their explanation from their special forms. But if there is an essential difference between both it is certainly not that of spontaneity, or self-motion*; the essential difference is, the absence of organic growth and psychic life in the one, and its presence in the other.†

* Spontaneity is generally pointed out as the essential and characteristic feature of psychic life in treatises on Free Will, where, as a rule, we meet with the vague expression that man is a " first cause." Those who employ this phrase mean, I suppose, that certain qualities of a man are the ground or *raison d'être* why to certain motives he responds, according to his character, with certain actions, so that all his actions must find their ultimate explanation (their ultimate *raison d'être*) in his character. This is true but the same holds good of all matter. The quality of being an acid is the ground why a certain substance combines with a base.

† Prof. Bunge, of Basel, and with him Alfred Binet, of Paris, call these

II.

CAN THE WORLD BE MECHANICALLY EXPLAINED?

IF causation is a law of motion every phenomenon of nature must have a mechanical aspect, and its process can in so far be reduced to mechanical laws. This being agreed upon, the question arises: "Can the world as a whole, and the life of the world, the actual existence of motion in the universe, be mechanically explained?"

Mechanics is the science of motion. Every motion can be expressed in terms of time and distance, *i. e.*, every motion is determined by its direction and velocity. Accordingly it can be computed with the assistance of mathematical and especially arithmetical rules. There is no motion, neither that of live organisms nor that of dead machines, which does not comply with mechanics: self-motion, as well as the transmitted motion of merely mechanical movements, is determined by the laws of mechanics. But this truism is not identical with an explanation of life from mechanical laws. Mechanics is not the *scientia ultima*, the ultimate *raison d'être* of natural phenomena. A mechanical explanation of the world would be possible, if the world consisted of purely mechanical phenomena. But purely mechanical phenomena do not even exist. Mechanical laws like pure mathematics have been abstracted from reality, ultimately resting upon the discrimination between form and matter, and represent one aspect only of real pro-cesses, *viz.*, the forms of motion. Purely mechanical

special features of organized life "vitalism." This usage of the word is fully justified if it is well distinguished from the old vitalism.

processes exist as little as mathematical points and lines.

The question so often proposed whether the existence of the world can be mechanically explained is therefore not justified. The question itself is wrong. A mechanical explanation is possible for every motion, for every single process that takes place. In all natural phenomena the transference of motion can be traced, the change from one form of motion into another can be shown. But a mechanical explanation is not applicable to solve the problem of the existence of motion. Existence, the existence of the world and the existence of motion, the sum total of the energy in the system of the universe, is a generalized statement of the fact of reality,—and the attempt to explain this fact mechanically as if existence at large were one special form or a single phenomenon, is based on a misconception. Science explains the different forms of existence, how one arises from the other, but not existence itself. Thus, also, mechanics explains the different forms of motion, how by transference one kind of motion originates from another kind; but motion itself can not be explained by mechanics.

Mr. Salter asks: "How can a body move itself?" The fact is, the body moves, whether it be some organized substance or an inorganic lump of matter; and our problem is: Does the body move because it possesses a certain quality which is intrinsic in the body, or does it move because it is pushed by a pressure from without? The problem is by no means definitely solved, so as to be verifiable by experiment; but there is no reason why in time it should not be solvable.

The most consistent solution from the standpoint

of materialism is perhaps the proposition of Le Sage and Mann.* Le Sage and Mann attempt to explain the chemical and physical motions of the atoms by the pressure of an all surrounding ether.

The ether-hypothesis of Le Sage is based on the consideration that matter is dead and the world a lifeless mechanism which must be set in motion by a pressure from the outside. It was invented in order to account for motion in inanimate masses. Le Sage thought to get rid of the idea of self-motion and of an animated universe. He attempted to explain the Universe mechanically and did not see that a mechanical explanation was impossible.

Our chief objection to Le Sage's mechanical explanation of life by a *vis a tergo* is, that it leaves the problem for the solution of which it was invented, untouched. If all the atoms of our body acted only because they are set in motion from the outside by the pressure of ether, feeling as well as consciousness would remain unexplained. In that case the ether would possess spontaneity, and not the atoms. If it were so, the ether around us and within us might feel and become conscious, but not the atoms that build up our body, and the problem of the origin of psychical life would be obscurer than ever. The origin of life would not be explained. On the contrary, by the assumption of dead and inert matter, life would become an impossibility.

Our opinion is, that the atoms possess spontaneity or the property of self-motion, which is akin to what in the higher forms of natural phenomena in the organic kingdom is called life. Self-motion is, therefore,

* In his pamphlet, *Der Atomaufbau in den chemischen Verbindungen.* Berlin: 1884. Heinicke.

life in a broader sense, and the phenomena which are
exhibited in protoplasm must ultimately find their explanation from the form of protoplasm as a special and
complicated instance of the simpler self-motions of inorganic substances.

The indisputable truth, that the universe with its
life and motion cannot be mechanically explained, has
induced some philosophers to speak of "hypermechanical" processes in nature as if motions existed that
could not be computed by mechanics. The word "hypermechanical" conveys the idea that it has to do with
mechanics of a higher degree, where the usual laws of
motion are annihilated and some incomprehensible
mysticism takes their place to account for certain peculiar phenomena of motion.

*   *   *

THE problem under discussion will find further
elucidation by a comparison of mechanics with other
formal sciences—especially logic. Logic is also an
abstract science. It treats of formal thought abstractly.
Thought has to comply, and does comply, with the
laws of logic. Of course thought does not always comply with the rules of logic; it drops often into illogical
fallacies. But that is no exception to the rule that
logic expresses the laws of formal thought abstractly;
for every error in real thought, every wrong conception in our mind, even every material disorder in our
brains, will lead to wrong conclusions which appear to
sound thinkers as illogical. This exception is no other
than that of a machine which is out of order so that
its mechanical result, in full accordance with the laws
of mechanics, is not what it ought to be.

Great philosophers have tried to understand the

universe logically. They were confident of constructing a universe out of pure thought and deducing existence (or being) from reason. This kind of philosophy, obviously erroneous and yet so natural in its time,
is called ontology (from ὤν, οὖσα, ὄν, ὄντος, being), because
real being or reality was derived from abstract being.
The most famous, and perhaps most consistent and
grandest, system of ontology is that of Hegel, who belongs to the generation following the era of Kant. Yet
so little was Kant understood at the time, that Hegel
grew prominent and more renowned than Kant ever
had been during his life. But the spirit of Kantian
criticism grew also; it grew like an oak, slowly but
strongly, and one sentence in his "Critique of Pure
Reason" so shook the system of Hegelian ontology
that it tumbled together like a house of cards. This
sentence of Kant's declares that "all knowledge *a
priori* is empty and cannot give information about
things."

Knowledge *a priori* Kant calls in other places 'formal' or 'transcendental' knowledge, and 'transcendental' in Kant's terminology does not denote anything transcendent or mysterious. Transcendental logic,
or pure logic, treats of the form of thought only, and abstracts form from the contents of thought altogether.
Therefore, pure reason, useful as it is for its purpose if
employed for criticism and as a regulator of correct
thinking, is useless for the purpose of ontology.

In opposition to the futile method of the ontologist,
those thinkers that instinctively felt that logic could
not answer the ultimate question about the existence
of the world—such men as understood the depth of
the problem, yet were unable to solve it—denounced
reason as altogether insufficient and even erroneous.

They spoke of a superior and divine reason in opposition to our weak human reason; as if reasons of different kind could exist.

The idea of 'hyper-mechanical motions' is shaped after the pattern of such 'supernatural reason,' which is conceived to stand in opposition to human reason. Hyper-mechanical is just as self-contradictory as hyper-logical, hyper-arithmetical, or hyper-mathematical, and all attempts to construe Rieman's ingenious idea of a curved space into a hyper-mathematical space-conception are vagaries.

If we meet with processes of motion which are so complicated that we cannot with our present knowledge discover in them the general law of motion, we need not despair of explaining them, by and by, from mechanical principles; even if they seem to contradict our basic concepts of mechanics, we must at last be able to find out that they are fundamentally the same phenomena and subject to the same laws.

Suppose that a man unfamiliar with the spirit of mathematics chanced to become acquainted with logarithms. Would he not be inclined to say that the rules of logarithms flatly contradict those of common arithmetic? Addition and substraction in the one system are represented by multiplication and division in the other; and again multiplication and division in the one represent raising the powers and extracting roots in the other. Logarithms will appear to him a kind of hyper-mathematics in which the theorems of common mathematics no longer hold good but are annihilated and substituted by other laws. Being in possession of the clew to the origin of logarithms from numbers, we know that this view is not justifiable. Logarithms are only one special and complex form of

arithmetic in which the common laws and basic concepts of arithmetic are not annihilated but modified
and specialized.

The unitary conception of the world keeps equally
aloof from ontology, which is an overvaluation of reason, and from mysticism, which is an undervaluation
of reason.

Comprehension has always to deal with forms.
Exclude from a conception form or the formal aspect
of things, and you exclude comprehensibility itself.

The order and form of the universe can be comprehended and investigated; but the universe, in its existence as a living whole, is not a special form of existence. There is, accordingly, nothing to be comprehended in existence in general. It is a matter of experience simply, to be stated as a fact.

By the form, for instance, of planets, we understand
their shape as globes (or rather as spheroids); by the
form of their motions we understand their paths, which
are conic sections. We cannot comprehend why planets materially exist, and why force exists inseparably
connected with matter. The material existence of planets, that their mass endowed with motion exists at all,
is a fact; but their existence as planets, why they exist
as spheroids, and why they travel in paths of conic
sections can very well be comprehended.

Intelligibility involves regularity of form, or order.
Chaos is unintelligible, but order can be comprehended.
The form of the universe being regulated by the laws
of form is the condition of its cosmical order and of
its intelligibility.

If the existence of matter and force in general
cannot be mechanically explained, because this problem is not included in the province of mechanics, we

are sure that every motion, every change of form can, at least theoretically, be explained from mechanics, the science of motion.

Mechanical laws explain mechanical phenomena, and mechanics is applicable to processes of motion only. Since existence at large, the existence of the world, is not a mechanical phenomenon, the question whether it can be mechanically explained, is not admissible.

III.

THE ELEMENTS EXPLAINABLE BY FORM.

THE materialistic, kinetic, and atomic conceptions of the world, as a rule, look upon matter as dead, and under the influence of this view the force of gravity has received the name of inertia. But matter is not dead or inert; its most generic quality is that of spontaneous motion and all the specific qualities of matter will eventually find their explanations from their special forms.

We may fairly suppose that matter in its most elementary shape is homogeneous. The world-substance, very probably, is continuous, and may in its very simplest form be identical with what our physicists call ether. The tenuity of ether is such that we cannot with our most delicate instruments verify its presence, and can only infer its existence from such physical phenomena as light and electricity. Whether it consists of discrete units we do not know; it is possible that it does. But if it indeed consists of minute units, single and uniform (I should call them with Leibnitz *monads*), it is certain that the world-substance possesses at the same time a continuity which places *all* these monads in relation to each other.

By continuity of the world-substance we mean that quality which binds all the ultimate units together so that the innumerable monads are not single independent individuals, but integral parts of the whole world—parts which by their positions mutually influence one another according to laws which can be ascertained and mathematically accounted for.

Two or more ether-monads combine into what is known as atoms, two or several atoms into molecules. The ether-monads are uniform, the atoms of the same combination of monads are uniform, and also the molecules of the same combination of atoms are uniform.

The combination of ether-monads into elementary atoms, I take to be comparable to the process of crystallization of minerals. Certain it is that it must take place according to mathematical laws. The atom must have a regular, perhaps a crystal-like shape; it must form a geometrical figure consisting of two or more monads.

This explanation of the problem seems to me the only possible solution which agrees with Mendeljeff's law of the periodicity of atomic weights. If the atoms possessed an individuality of their own, ultimately due to material qualities, if their properties were not due to their form but to their substance, it would be very strange if not miraculous that one atom of oxygen is so exactly like unto every other atom of oxygen. What can be the cause of this, so far as we can judge, absolute identity of all atoms of the same element? Can it really be an ultimate and substantial quality which inheres in it from all eternity ? If it were, we should be disposed to believe *a priori* (if we did not know anything to the contrary) that no two atoms would be exactly like each other, and that innumerable elements would be found in nature.   Facts disprove this.

The absolute identity of two atoms of the same element can be reasonably explained only if we consider their identity as a sameness of *form*. Let us suppose that several (perhaps two) uniform monads of the homogeneous ether, by a certain pressure, at a certain degree of heat, and under other certain conditions yet unknown, crystallize, as it were, into a certain geometrical figure which chemists now call an atom of Hydrogen. Under other conditions thirty-two monads ($2 \times 16 = 32$) will combine into another geometrical figure, which would be an atom of Oxygen. The substance in the two monads of the Hydrogen atom and the thirty-two monads of the Oxygen atom is supposed to be the same ether; but the combinations are different. If we knew what the geometrical shapes of the atoms were, we would be able to state why in the one case two and in the other thirty-two monads are required to make up one atom.

If a difference of the various elements is a difference of form only, we can account for their uniformity in all regions of the universe as easily as we account for the spheroidal shapes of the heavenly bodies and for their paths in conic sections. Moreover, if such is the case, we understand why the number of the elements is so limited, and why the atomic weights of the elements are so regular and invariable. Perhaps if we had a sufficiently powerful lens we could arithmetically compute and geometrically demonstrate why the atomic weight of sodium, for example, is exactly 23, why at the same time an element of one or a few unit-weights more or less cannot exist, and why the periodicity of the atomic weights cannot be otherwise.

Perhaps such a *demonstratio ad oculos* of the fundamental chemical law would be as simple as to show
that the tetrahedron has four, the octahedron eight,
the tetrahexahedron twenty-four equal faces of equilateral triangles, that the cube's faces are squares and
those of the dodecahedron, pentagons. We, then,
should see why the atomic weights of the elements
form progressive series, as 7.02, 23, 39.14, 63, 85.2; why
the elements can be classified in families as it were,
and why in the same family atoms of intermediate
weights are as impossible as, *e. g.*, a heptahedron with
congruent faces is a geometrical impossibility.*

While the combinations of the monads into atoms
are limited to the comparatively small number of
about seventy elements, it is natural that the possibilities of molecular combinations increase immeasur-
ably; and the possible combinations of molecules into
specific substances must be infinite.

IV.

MACHINES AND ORGANISMS.

WHILE we are compelled to recognize in the atomic
combinations of molecules the features of living spontaneous action, we would not consider a conglomeration
or a chemical mixture, as an interaction of live relations. A piece of marl, or sandstone, or granite, is an
unorganized *mixtum compositum* of parts that possess
a mere fortuitous coherence without a living interaction among themselves. A piece of stone as such is
not a living thing. It is a dead aggregate, whatever
life its parts may possess.

* For further explanation of the Periodic Law compare *Wurz*, " The Atomic
Theory," Eng. Transl., pp. 158, 159, 163 and 170; and *Dr. Lothar Meyer, Die
Modernen Theorien der Chemie*, pp. 139-141.

Similarly a machine, although its parts are systematized for a special purpose, cannot be said to be alive. It does not possess the life of an organism. Its particles, the wood and the iron, will, under certain conditions, exhibit the same self-motion of which all matter is possessed. The molecules of wood, for instance, will embrace the oxygen of a flame as fervidly as a lover rushes into the arms of his mistress. But the machine as a whole does not possess the life of an organism. Its motion is no spontaneity of an organic interaction of its parts, but a mere transference of movement by push and pressure. Living bodies have been compared to machines because the motions of life-structures take place according to the same mechanical laws as the motions of machines. And, indeed, living bodies are mechanisms just as much as machines. But there is a difference. The difference is that they are living machines. In a machine the motion is transmitted by expansive pressure from the fire-place and boiler to other parts of the machine. In an organism the smallest particle has a fire-place and boiler of its own from which it derives motor power. Its parts possess a spontaneous and mutual interaction, producing a systematic communication among them, which grows out of their own intrinsic qualities into a natural unity; whereas the unity of a machine is that of an artificial composition.

. V.

ORGANIZED AND PSYCHICAL LIFE.

IT is contended that while the problem of the Descent of Man may have been solved, the problem of Life remains unsolved, because the origin of protoplasm is not yet demonstrated.

This is true; but it must be remarked that the problem to be solved is rather the " origin of the form of protoplasm " than the " origin of life." The spontaneity of living substance is found in the kingdom of inorganic nature also. A base and an acid rush toward each other and combine in the form of a salt. As soon as we know what the molecular forms of bases and acids are like, we can hope to be able to comprehend why they combine into substances of a new form, which have the properties of salts. If the science of molecular chemistry (which does not yet exist) should succeed in a discovery of this kind, the problem of the formation of salt crystals would be solved and the affinity of bases and acids would have found its explanation. But the problem why the atoms of a certain shape fit to atoms of another shape, is different from the other problem: Why do the atoms rush towards each other at all?

Although the origin of organized life has not yet been sufficiently explained, the characteristic feature of organized life is to some extent determined. In the vegetative kingdom it has been called constructive metabolism in so far as plants through the process of osmose convert the relatively simple compounds of inorganic substances into protoplasm, in the complex structure of which energy is stored. The characteristic feature of animal life is not only the procreation of protoplasma freighted with energy, but chiefly the expenditure of this energy. The process of life in the cells of animal organisms therefore exhibits two essential phases—the one is constructive of energy (anabolism), the other by a process of decomposition sets energy free (katabolism) and is thus productive of the special features of animal life, particularly heat, free motion, and sensation.

Animal life is a continuous process, a constant building up and breaking down. " There are two series of events, two staircases, as it were, of chemical transformation,—one an ascending staircase of synthetic, anabolic processes through which the pabulum, consisting of several substances, some of them already complex and unstable, is built up into the still more complex and still more unstable protoplasm; the other a descending staircase, consisting of a series of katabolic processes giving rise to substances of decreasing complexity and increasing stability."*

The origin of psychic life has always been the greatest stumbling-block to scientists and philosophers. It appeared so totally different from other natural phenomena that it was considered as something that must have been introduced from other, unknown and more spiritual, spheres. The existence of psychic life is indeed the corner-stone of dualism. Dualism will prevail so long as feeling, sensation, and consciousness are considered as something foreign to our world— something that has not grown from, and does not stand in connection with, the elements of reality. But if we

---

* Encyclopædia Britannica, vol. xix, p. 19, Physiology, where Prof. E. Hering's theory is explained.

bear in mind that physical and chemical processes can
not be explained as inert movements produced through
some machine-like, mechanical transference by pressure or outward push upon dead particles of matter—if
physical and chemical processes are recognized (as
they actually are) to be live spontaneous self-motions—
we can see no theoretical difficulty (however great the
practical difficulties may be) to the assumption that
biological and with them psychological processes originate from the same elements and are a special and
more complex form merely of natural phenomena in
general.   Even a century ago, every physicist would
have spurned the idea that heat and light were modes
of motion only, that they can be produced out of any
other kind of motion.   The procreation of psychic life
from the life of spontaneously moving atoms seems to
me not less wonderful than that light is born out of
night, when two dark bodies, meeting in their paths,
mutually arrest each other in their courses and change
their motion of progression in space into molecular
motion.

The question arises, If the life of organisms is a
special form of life in a broader sense, why did our
scientists fail to produce organisms artificially, and
why did they despair of creating the organized life of
protoplasm?

The answer is obvious if we bear in mind that all
organized life is the result of memory.   Our most
powerful microscopes, even if they were a thousand
times improved, would be still insufficient to discover
even the grossest vestiges that constitute, in protoplasm, the physiological aspect of memory.   To read a
sonata from the tinfoil of a phonograph must be easy
in comparison to a discovery of the traces of memory

produced in organized substance. And if our scientists were able to produce living substance in which at least the process of metabolism takes place and which will preserve the traces of memory, the discovery would be grand but we would be in possession of the mere potentiality of organized life. In order to produce an organism as low in the scale of life as a moner, we would have to expose it to all the irritations and experiences through which the moner has naturally passed; and we are not sure as to how many thousand years are required for this process, and whether, if it were artificially abbreviated, the same result could be attained.

All organized life and especially all psychical life has evolved from the general life of the universe. The development from the most primitive life of self-moving matter, which obtained in the igneous state of our planet, to the expression of intellectual human activity, forms one great and uninterrupted continuity. The ground and basis of this continuity is the conscious and still more so the unconscious memory of organized matter in all its many differentiated forms. Science has solved many problems of psychology, physiology, and biology, but the solutions have always been such as account for certain forms of life. The evolution-theory, so far as it goes, explains how the human form and other animal forms have developed from the simplest forms of protoplasm. Every living particle of man's body is protoplasm of a certain form; and science, when showing how the human form must have developed, has solved the problem of the Descent of Man.

It is a very strange fact that protoplasm, being a very complex compound, exhibits in its first stage a singular sameness wherever it is found. This indicates that here also the solution of the problem must be looked for in the structure (*i. e.*, the form) of protoplasm. The shaping of forms follows mathematical modes; and unalterable regularity is always dependent upon the laws of form. Mathematics (the science of form) will explain the nature of the elements; but mathematics must do more, it must also explain the problem of the origin of physiological and psychical life.

CONCLUSION.

THE existence of life being a fact, and all supernatural or dualistic theories being inadmissible, we see no simpler solution of the problem than that of considering life in its broadest sense as an immanent property of matter. As such, it remains what it ever has been—a fact ascertainable by experience. All explanations of the higher life of plants and animals will have to be confined to demonstrating how the higher forms of life originate from uniform life by showing the continuity of all life and the development from its simplest forms of spontaneous motion to its highest form, which in the human will, rises to heroic heights.

Monism, by accepting the idea that nature is alive, does not return to the old mythological standpoint. The characteristic feature of mythology is the fact that things are considered as animated *like ourselves.* The savage has sufficient power of generalization, as Mr. Spencer would express it, to see the similarity between ourselves and things. But he lacks the power of discrimination, which is indispensable to scientific investigation. He cannot appreciate the difference be-

tween the babbling brook and a prattling girl: in the
murmur of the water he hears the voice of a nymph.
Monism, by explaining the truth that lies at the bottom
of mythology, will afford the only means of liberating
our minds from its errors; for mythological errors, it is
true, are lurking everywhere in our conceptions and
in our words.   It would be impossible to clear language of mythological comparisons and similes without sweeping it entirely out of existence.   If we tried
to use language that is free from mythology, we would
be obliged to invent a new Volapük—a language that
has no historical development, that is not infected with
the errors of the past, yet will be understood nowhere.

Is it necessary to create such a language, a philosophical Volapük?   Probably not.   It is sufficient to
show the traces of mythology and to explain their origin.   We still speak of sunrise and yet we know it is
the earth by its rotation that causes the appearance of
the sun on special parts of its surface.   We know it,
and every child now knows it, without taking offense
at the inadequacy of the expression.

We make bold to say that there is no word in any
language which is not from some point of view an in-
adequate, or a mythological, or a dualistic expression.
If we employ the term life in its broadest sense as
spontaneity or self-motion, we are conscious of using
a mythological expression.   The same is true of such
words as affinity in Chemistry, attraction and repul-
sion in Physics, of the sexes in Botany and of innumerable other cases.

Anthropomorphism is not only allowable and justifiable, it is even indispensable to a proper comprehension of phenomena external to us.   Man is a part
of nature and man's whole existence must be under-

stood as a special form and combination of certain natural phenomena. A direct knowledge of nature is given to us in our consciousness only; and this con sciousness must be used in order to interpret the other phenomena of nature. Accordingly, the natural development of human comprehension will lead us through anthropomorphism, of which science will free us step by step, from which, however, we never shall nor can be, severed entirely; for there is a truth in anthropomorphism which is fully explained by the doctrine of monism that Nature is one great and living whole of which man is a part—such a part as contains in its form the quintessence of nature's life.

Psychical phenomena, such as take place in our consciousness, so far as we are now familiar with them, must be limited to organized life. But since the atoms, in spontaneous self-motion, exercise the faculty of choice, it seems that a time will come, although it is not near at hand, when we shall find ourselves obliged to use the term 'psychical' in a broader sense and speak of a psychology of atoms and molecules.

CAUSE, REASON, AND END.

EVERY phenomenon has a cause (αἰτία), which is a motion that starts the whole process ; every phenomenon takes place according to a certain law (νόμος), which explains its *raison d'être*, the reason why the process takes place. Every phenomenon takes a certain course, and its motion results in a new state of things. This result is called the aim or end (τέλος) of the phenomenon. If the motion is a conscious will, the aim or end pursued is called the purpose. Accordingly there are three aspects under which phenomena may be considered ; the inquiry into their causes is the *ætiological*, into their laws the *nomological*, into their ends the *teleological* method. None of them is sufficient by itself ; thorough investigations have to employ all three.

The teleological method is erroneously based upon the idea that the aims or ends of physical processes have been determined beforehand by an omniscient demiurge. Such conceptions are to be excluded as dualistic and have found their refutation in former essays.

The teleological method, in so far as it is employed for teaching the ought of aspirations to rational beings, is called *ethological*. As such it investigates the course of phenomena and the state of things to which they lead ; and in order to produce higher forms of life and further the progress of humanity it lays down certain rules or maxims which appear to us as religious commandments or ethical norms.

THE IDEA OF ABSOLUTE EXISTENCE.

I.

THE VEIL OF MAYA.

THE Hindoo Sages compared the world, as it appears to our senses, to a veil—the veil of Maya—which lies upon our eyes and thus shrouds the true aspect of things. And the same view, with comparatively slight modifications, is repeated in the philosophy of Plato. In a poetical passage in the "Republic," the Grecian philosopher compares human knowledge to the condition of men who sit in a cavern facing the wall opposite the entrance; being bound to the spot since birth by chains about their feet and neck. They cannot look around, they cannot see the persons and things passing by behind them, but they see their shadows on the wall opposite and imagine that these appearances are the real things.

The view that natural processes are not actual realities, but mere shadows of invisible existences behind them, has been revived often since, and must be considered even to-day as the philosophy of our time; and only gradually a new conception of the world is rising that looks upon natural processes, the phenomena so-called, as the positive facts of knowledge. The expression ' phenomenon ' means ' appearance ;' the word has been introduced and is now generally

employed as a synonym of 'natural process' because
the Hindoo conception of the sham-existence of reality was, some time ago, all but universal.

Immanuel Kant, in his Critique of Pure Reason,
often speaks of " the thing of itself," and he says that
we cannot have any positive knowledge of it. This was
very discouraging, but it afforded those who paraded
a Faust-like thirst for knowledge yet did not have the
strength to devote a life of patient labor to earnest
thought and research, an easy means of satisfying their
yearning. Our knowledge is but relative, they said to
themselves, and it is impossible to conceive the Absolute; the Absolute is the Unconditioned, and to our
limited cognition it must be unknowable. If we could
comprehend it, we would be omniscient like God, but
as matters are, we are limited to the phenomenal world
and must confess with Faust:

> " That which one does not know, one needs to use;
> And what one knows, one uses never."

If the absolute is incomprehensible, all our knowledge is vain, and worst of all, we can never hope to
know anything about God and about our soul. Is not
our soul our absolute self, the thing of itself which
manifests itself in our existence? And is not God, the
absolute of the universe, manifested in all the innumerable phenomena of nature? God and soul viewed
from this standpoint, are unknowabilities.

Kant goes beyond this standpoint. The concepts
'Soul' and 'God,' as absolute existences or things of
themselves, are paralogisms of pure reason. We have
arrived at these ideas by a fallacy. We experience in
our consciousness a consecutive series of sensations or
thoughts, but from this fact we cannot infer the existence of a 'consciousness without its contents' as a thing

of itself. The world is an orderly arranged whole, but from this fact we cannot infer that a transcendent God is the author of this order. Kant adds in his Critique of Practical Reason, that although the ideas of God and soul are paralogisms, we should regulate our lives as if they existed; we should act as if we had a soul and as if a God existed—a just judge to reward the good and punish the evil.

These ideas of Kant have become popular and the unknowability of the thing of itself contributed greatly to the growth of agnostic thought in England.

II.

AGNOSTICISM AND PHENOMENALISM.

THE name 'agnostic' was invented by Professor Huxley for the avowed purpose of appeasing obtrusive persons, who bored him with questions as to his belief or disbelief in the existence of God, and the immortality of the soul. ' Prof. Huxley states the facts as follows:

"Some twenty years ago, or thereabouts,* I invented the word 'Agnostic' to denote people who, like myself, confess themselves to be hopelessly ignorant concerning a variety of matters, about which metaphysicians and theologians, both orthodox and heterodox, dogmatize with the utmost confidence; and it has been a source of some amusement to me to watch the gradual acceptance of the term and its correlate, Agnosticism. * * * Thus it will be seen that I have a sort of patent right in 'Agnostic.' It is my trade-mark and I am entitled to say that I can state authentically what was originally meant by Agnosticism. Agnosticism is the essence of science, whether ancient or modern. It simply means that a man shall not say he knows or believes that which he has

* These lines were written by Prof. Huxley in 1884.

no scientific grounds for professing to know or believe. * * * I have no doubt that scientific criticism will prove destructive to the forms of supernaturalism which enter into the constitution of existing religions. On trial of any so-called miracle, the verdict of science is 'not proven.' But Agnosticism will not forget that existence, motion, and law-abiding operation in nature are more stupendous miracles than any recounted by the mythologies and that there may be things, not only in the heavens and earth, but beyond the intelligible universe, which 'are not dreamt of in our philosophy.' The theological 'gnosis' would have us believe that the world is a conjurer's house; the anti-theological 'gnosis' talks as if it were a 'dirt-pie' made by two blind children, Law and Force. Agnosticism simply says that *we know nothing of what may be beyond phenomena.*"*

In another passage the great English biologist states his views concerning the immortality of the soul:

"If anybody says that consciousness cannot exist except in relation of cause and effect with certain organic molecules I must ask how he knows that; and, if he says it can, I must put the same question. And I am afraid that, like jesting Pilate, I shall not think it worth while (having but little time before me) to wait for an answer." †

If, with the Hindoo, we regard natural phenomena as a veil, we may compare the scientist to a man who dares to lift that veil, and reveals to us part of the hidden truth. But even so, many Agnostics say, our knowledge must remain incomplete. While we inquire into the manifestations of forces, while we observe how they operate, we shall never be able to know what Matter is and what Force is. Their relations in the phenomenal world may be knowable, but their absolute existence is unknowable.

In answer to this view we must state that there is no absolute force, no force of itself. The so-called 'phenomena ' of forces are the realities, and the differ-

---

* The *italics* are ours.
† Prof. Huxley in the *Fortnightly Review*, Dec. 1886.

ent forces, such as heat, electricity, etc., are abstract conceptions in which we embrace all the natural processes of one kind. Not 'force' and 'matter' are things to be comprehended; they in their turn have been invented to comprehend phenomena. They do not go beyond phenomena but simply classify and arrange them, in order to comprehend them all together, if possible, in one unitary and consistent system.

Prof. Huxley, while confessing himself to be an Idealist, in an address on Descartes's 'Discourse,' introduces at the same time the mysticism which naturally follows from the principle of Agnosticism that "we know nothing of what may be beyond phenomena." Prof. Huxley says:

" If I say that *impenetrability* is a property of matter, all that I can really mean is that the consciousness I call *extension* and the consciousness I call *resistance*, constantly accompany one another. Why and how they are thus related is a mystery; and if I say that thought is a property of matter, all that I can mean is that, actually or possibly, the consciousness of extension and that of resistance accompany all other sorts of consciousness. But as in the former case, why they are thus associated, is *an insoluble mystery.*"*

The concepts 'Impenetrability,' 'Extension,' and 'Resistance,' as they appear in our consciousness, are abstracts which denote certain qualities to be met with in our experience. If the spheres of two abstracts cover, either entirely or in part, the same ground, then as a matter of course the two ideas will always (either entirely or in part) appear to be associated. We form the abstract idea of matter by noting the qualities of all the different kinds of matter, dropping their individual features and retaining those only which they possess in common. Two qualities of matter (the two features which all matters have in common) are generalized

* *Italics* are ours.

under the names of mass and volume. Mass and volume, both being abstracts of the same object, *viz.*, of matter, it is but natural that they will always be associated, the one with the other. According to Prof. Huxley's method we should say: Why the consciousness I call ' mass ' and the consciousness I call ' volume ' constantly accompany one another is an insoluble mystery.

If we take the agnostic standpoint, the whole world becomes enigmatic and even such a fact as that the consciousness we call ' liquid ' constantly accompanies the consciousness we call ' fluid ' would appear as a profound mystery.

Professor Bain shows in his " Practical Essays," p. 56, that the word 'mysterious' has sense only if used in opposition to what is plain and intelligible :

" When we are told * * * that *everything is mysterious;* that the simplest phenomenon in nature—the fall of a stone, the swing of a pendulum, the continuance of a ball shot in the air—are wonderful, marvelous, miraculous, our understanding is confounded; there being then nothing plain at all, there is nothing mysterious. * * * If all phenomena are mysterious, nothing is mysterious; if we are to stand aghast in amazement because three times four is twelve, what phenomenon can we take as the type of the plain and the intelligible?"

Prof. Huxley in answer to two onslaughts on his position (one by Dr. Wace from the standpoint of orthodox theology, the other by Mr. Harrison, the defender of the Comtean Positive Philosophy), most ably and, indeed, successfully defends his agnosticism.* It is almost superfluous to state that we concur

* *Nineteenth Century* February, 1889. Prof. Huxley informs us in this article that Sir William Hamilton's essay " On the Philosophy of the Unconditioned " which he read when a boy had stamped upon his mind the strong conviction that the limitation of our faculties in a great number of cases renders real answers to certain questions not merely actually impossible but theoretically inconceivable.

with him wherever he objects to the antiquated belief of demonology. When he characterizes agnosticism as the principle 'Try all things and hold fast by that which is good' and when he identifies it with "the axiom that every man should be able to give a reason for the faith that is in him," we heartily and fully agree with his agnosticism; our objection holds *only* in so far as Professor Huxley says "that we know nothing of what may be beyond phenomena."

III.

GŒTHE'S MONISM.

AGNOSTICISM, in so far as it declares that we know nothing of what lies beyond phenomena, divides the world into two parts: One of them consists of knowable phenomena, and the other is the realm of the absolute, of the unknowable. The former are things as they appear, and the latter, things of themselves. The phenomenal is merely the outside appearance of some mysterious inside kernel. The famous naturalist Haller expressed this opinion in the following lines:

> "Nature's 'within' from mortal mind
> Must ever lie concealed.
> Thrice blessed e'en he to whom she has
> Her outer shell revealed."

Goethe who could not be reconciled to this view which splits nature in twain and places us outside of nature as if we were locked out from her secrets forever, replied to Haller's verses with the following poem:

" Nature's ' within ' from mortal mind"
Philistine, sayest thou,
" Must ever lie concealed?"
To me, my friend, and to my kind
Repeat this not. We trow
Where'er we are that we
Within must always be.

*" Thrice blessed e'en he to whom she has
Her outer shell revealed?"*
This saying sixty years I heard
Repeated o'er and o'er,
And in my soul I cursed the word,
Yet secretly I swore.
Some thousand thousand times or more
Unto myself I witness bore:
"Gladly gives Nature all her store,
She knows not kernel, knows not shell,
For she is all in one.
                    But thou,
Examine thou thine own self well
Whether thou art kernel or art shell."

IV.

PHENOMENA AND NOUMENA.

KANT'S philosophy and especially his doctrine of
the unknowability of ' things of themselves ' have
given, it is true, a great ascendency to agnosticism
and at the same time to the mysticism of antiquated
orthodoxy. Nevertheless the spirit of Kantian thought
is far from both, and it leads neither to the one nor to
the other of these deadly antagonists, but to a unitary
conception of the world on the ground of positive
facts—a conception which may be called Positivism,* or Monism.

* The introduction of the word "Positivism" into philosophy is the merit
of M. Auguste Comte. Although we cannot accept M. Comte's conception of
Positivism, we gratefully adopt the name, which, as a synonym of Monism,
is a strong and expressive term.

Kant's philosophy, we must bear in mind, is not a system but a method. He tried to avoid the faults of Wolf's Dogmatism on the one side, and of Hume's Skepticism on the other. Thus, he proposed what he called Criticism. He did not offer a plain and outspoken solution of the problems, but he did the work to enable others to solve them: he formulated the problems.

Kant discusses (in Chap. III of the Transcendental Doctrine of the Faculty of Judgment) the "discrimination of all objects as phenomena and noumena." Phenomena are the natural processes which affect our senses (*Sinneswesen*). They are the data of our experience and provide the building materials out of which we create our conceptions of things. Noumena, in contradistinction to phenomena, are pure ideas (*Verstandeswesen*). Kant used the word "noumenon" in its original sense. It is the present passive participle of νοεῖν 'to think' and means 'something thought' or 'a creation of our mind.'

The word noumenon is not only wrongly used by many philosophers of to-day, but our dictionaries also present a wrong definition. Webster says:

"*Nou'-me-non* [Gr. νούμενον, the thing perceived, p. pr. pass. of νοεῖν, to perceive, νοῦς, the mind,] (*Metaph.*) The of itself unknown and unknowable rational object, or *thing in itself*, which is distinguished from the *phenomenon* in which it occurs to apprehension, and by which it is interpreted and understood:—so used in the philosophy of Kant and his followers."

"νούμενον," here, is a misprint for νοούμενον. Accordingly the pronunciation *no-oo'-menon* is preferable to Webster's pronunciation *noo'-me-non*. The latter is commonly used, but the former is the only correct pronunciation.

Webster's translation of the original Greek word as "the thing perceived" is wrong. The noumenon is the thing *thought,* while the phenomenon must be called the thing *perceived.* The Greek verb νοεῖν does not mean "to perceive," as Webster states, but to think.

Such concepts as God, World, and Soul are pure ideas according to Kant, therefore he calls them noumena. Things of themselves (whether they exist or not) are not objects of sensation, they are creations of our mind; therefore they are noumena. Accordingly, not the noumenon is a thing in itself, as Webster states, but just the opposite is true: The thing of itself is a noumenon. In other words, Kant does not say: Pure ideas (such as God and Soul) are things of themselves; but on the contrary he says: All things of themselves, the concepts God and Soul included, are pure ideas; they are not objects of sense perception.*

Concerning noumena or pure thoughts Kant emphatically declares that they have no significance unless they have reference to the phenomenal. *i. e.,* to the real sensations of our experience.

Kant says: †

" Everything which the understanding draws from itself, without borrowing from experience, it nevertheless possesses only for the behoof and use of experience. * * *

"That the understanding, therefore, cannot make of its *a priori* principles, or even of its conceptions, other than an empirical use, is a proposition which leads to the most important results.

"A transcendental use is made of a conception in a fundamental

* We discuss Webster's mistake thus fully because the errors that are perpetuated in dictionaries are highly misleading and injurious. One wrong idea of fundamental importance imbibed in younger years produces a great confusion, of which weaker minds will never perhaps be able to free themselves.

† Translation by Meiklejohn.

proposition or principle, when it is referred to things *in general* and considered as things *in themselves;* an empirical use, when it is referred merely to *phenomena*, that is, to objects of a possible *experience.* That the latter use of a conception is the only admissible one, is evident from the reasons following.

" For every conception are requisite, firstly, the logical form of a conception (of thought) in general; and, secondly, the possibility of presenting to this an object to which it may apply. Failing this latter, it has no sense, and is utterly void of content, although it may contain the logical function for constructing a conception from certain data

" Now an object cannot be given to a conception otherwise than by intuition, and, even if a pure intuition antecedent to the object is *a priori* possible, this pure intuition can itself obtain objective validity only from empirical intuition, of which it is itself but a form. All conceptions, therefore, and with them all principles, however high the degree of their *a priori* possibility, relate to empirical intuitions, that is to data towards a possible experience. Without this they possess no objective validity, but are a mere play of imagination or of understanding with images or notions. * * * -

" The conceptions of mathematics would have no significance, if we were not always able to exhibit their significance in and by means of phenomena (empirical objects). * * *

" The pure categories are of no use at all, when separated from sensibility."

In the second edition of his Critique of Pure Reason, Kant has inserted a few paragraphs, in which he discusses " the causes why we (not yet satisfied with the substratum of sensation) have added the noumena to the phenomena." " We have learned," he says, " that sensation does not perceive things of themselves, but as they appear to us in accordance with our subjective condition." Now, as they cannot be appearances of themselves, we suppose that something must correspond to it, something which is independent of sensation.

Kant distinguishes two kinds of noumena. Noumena, in the positive sense, he defines to be those that are supposed to have originated in a non-sensuous intuition, and declares that they are inadmissible:

"We in this case assume a peculiar mode of intuition, an intellectual intuition, to wit, which does not, however, belong to us, of the very possibility of which we have no notion."

Noumena, in the negative sense, Kant calls things in so far as we abstract from sensation altogether; they are pure ideas, merely formal thought. They are not only admissible but for certain purposes necessary.

" A noumenon considered as merely problematical, is not only admissible but even indispensable. * * * It is a negative extension of reason. * * * We limit sensation by giving to things of themselves (in so far as they are not considered as phenomena) the name of noumena."

" The division of objects into phenomena and noumena, and of the world into a *mundus sensibilis* and *intelligibilis* is therefore quite inadmissible in a positive sense (although conceptions do certainly admit of such a division); for the latter class of noumena have no determinate object corresponding to them, and cannot therefore possess objective validity.

* * * " After all, the possibility of such noumena is quite incomprehensible, and beyond the sphere of phenomena all is for us a mere void. * * * What, therefore, we call noumenon, must be understood by us as such in a *negative* sense."

Thus the question whether our reason, in addition to its admitted empirical use, can be employed in a transcendental way to noumena as objects, is answered by Kant in the negative.

The root of false noumenalism, it seems to us, must be sought in language. It is a misconception of the nature of words which leads us to think that things are absolute existences, being independent of, and distinct from their qualities. If we keep a clear conception, however, of the way words have arisen, and of the purpose they serve, we shall not fall into this dualism that believes in an absolutely unknowable world supposed to be hid behind the knowable world of sense-phenomena.

Words are, so to speak, bundles of percepts. If we pull single percepts out, the bundle is still a bundle; but if we take away all, there is no bundle left, there is nothing remaining that made the bundle a bundle; we have left only an empty nothing. If we take away from a thing all the properties that we are accustomed to comprehend by a word, there is left the meaningless word, a mere sound, the bare string with which the bundle was tied together.

The world is not in a rigid unchangeable state, but in a continuous flux. Yet knowledge becomes possible only when we fix certain percepts and give them relative stability. The faculty of fixing and retaining percepts, namely memory, is therefore the ladder that leads us upwards to a higher spiritual existence; it affords the mechanical means of gaining a firm foothold in the course of eternal changes.

It is as if we sat in an express train and were looking at the landscape flitting by us. The picture, taken as a whole, swims indistinctly before our eyes. If we wish to get a clear idea of the situation, we must allow the eye to rest on some one object, neglecting the others. This we do, in viewing nature, by the concept, *i. e.*, by the word. Words are the instruments by which we fix, in symbols of sound, certain classes of events, perceptions, or experiences; giving them a relative stability despite the universal change of things. In this rests the importance of words, for it is only in this way that we can at all separate a group of occurrences from the course of nature, in order to scrutinize them closely, and to understand them. We must always

bear the fact in mind that the element of stability
that seems to be present in many words, is a fiction
designed to serve a definite purpose.   Absolute rest
does not exist.   Things are in a constant flux, and if we
give our words and concepts a relative fixity, we
must nevertheless not seek in them eternal existences,
or absolute entities, as did Plato, in his 'Ideas.'

v.

THE ONENESS OF THE PHENOMENAL AND THE NOUMENAL.

WHAT we call things, what we call our personality,
our Self, our Ego, are merely abstract concepts that we
have formed for the purpose of distinguishing them
from other things.   Words serve the practical purpose
of orientation among the innumerable phenomena of
nature.   Absolutely considered, and independent of
their properties, things neither exist, nor do we ourselves.   Properties are parts of a thing, abstracted
from it in thought.   Some, and in fact very many, of
these properties are only separable in thought, and not
in reality, from things; while the totality of all properties constitutes the thing entire.   Most of the words,
by which we designate things, are furthermore shifting
concepts.   We retain the same word, even when parts
or properties of a thing, it may be, have fallen away
or when new ones are added.   The rose-bush in the
garden continues the same rose-bush, even after we
have ·engrafted another species into its stem; it has
merely lost certain properties and acquired new ones.
A hat without a band and trimming is still a hat, and
an old hat with a new band and new trimming con-

tinues to be the same hat to us. Only when the change made is very great do we cease to designate the object by the old name.

We ourselves remain ourselves, although continually changing, in body as well as in mind. Of our world of ideas, various parts fade away, or are wholly forgotten, while with new experiences new thoughts continually grow from the old ones.

In order completely to understand a thing, we must know it in its relation to other things. The character of a table is constituted not only by its shape, but also by its purpose to serve people as a table. Without this purpose, properly considered, a table would *not* be a table. A stone, for instance, that has been accidentally shaped into the form of a table by the grinding action of a glacier, is no table. The surroundings in which a table serves the purpose of a table, thus belong to the table as a property which we cannot separate from it. We must learn to understand everything, therefore, not as the expression of something having a separate, absolute existence, that lies concealed behind its realities, but as a part of the All.

Our bodies, of themselves, and apart from all else, would not be able to exist. Without the pressure of the atmosphere, we would burst asunder, while the air surrounding us belongs most intimately to our lungs. A recent scientist has called the kitchen an extension of our chewing and digesting apparatuses. And correctly. But also the fields upon which grow the corn that miller and baker convert into bread for us, belong to our Selves. In reality, the whole world is a part of our being, and the manifestation of our existence is conditioned wholly by the relations in which we stand to the outer world.

This holds good not only of our physical, but still more so of our spiritual existence. Our soul is made up of perceptions and ideas. The objects of our perceptions and our thoughts acquire thereby a relation to our Self; they become parts of the Self, which in the event of a change also transform the corresponding parts of the Self.

The closer the connection is in which a thing stands to us, the more it appears as a part of our being. The skilled violin-player feels his violin, as though it were a part of his body. He controls it, indeed, as an acrobat does his limbs. A benumbed limb which no longer pains, on the contrary, appears as a foreign body that does not belong to us. The captain of a company conducts his troops, as an engineer controls his engine. The engine becomes a part of the engine-driver, the company a part of the captain, and the audience a part of the speaker. Everything it is true, rests upon reciprocity. The speaker in his turn is a part of the audience. Language is the bond of union; in language speaker and audience are one. The speaker must speak the language of his audience, and the audience must understand the language that he speaks. So the engineer is part of the locomotive and he must be familiar with it; in other words, a picture of the locomotive must exist as a living nerve-structure in his brain.

Although we are, in fact, distinct individuals, distinguished from each other by an "I" or a "you," by a "he" or a "she"; yet when closely scrutinized, the "you" of our friends and enemies is a part our own Self. In every way the "I," "you," "he," "she," and "we" are parts of a great whole; and human society with its social and political institutions, with its ethical ideas and ideals, is only possible because these "you's" are but little distinct from the "I's." That our life and property in general is safe, that we buy and sell, marry and are given in marriage, that the laws are observed, and that in ordinary circumstances we hold intercourse with one another mutually trusting in our honest intentions; that, too, we struggle and compete with one another and try our best to maintain our places in the universal aspiration onward:—all this is only possible because we are parts of the same humanity and the children of the same epoch, possessing the same ideas of right and wrong, and bearing within ourselves in a certain sense the same souls.

Could some evil spirit, over night, change our souls into those of savages and cannibals, or even into those of the robber-knights of the middle ages, all our sacred laws, all our constables, all the police power of the State would be of no avail: we would inevitably sink back to the state of civilization in which those people existed. But could a God ennoble our souls, so that the sense of right and reason became still more purified in every heart, then better things would result spontaneously and much misery and error would vanish from the earth.

VI.

GOD AS THE MORAL LAW.

AND the God that can accomplish that, lives indeed —not beyond the clouds, but here on earth, in the heart of every man and woman. An absolute God exists as little as an absolute soul or an absolute thing. We no longer believe in ghosts, and an absolute God, just as an absolute soul is not distinguishable at all from a ghost.

By God we understand the order of the world, that makes harmony, evolution, aspiration, and morality possible. This God is no transcendental thing, existing of itself, enthroned above the clouds; he is immanent, and lives in the hearts of men as their good-will, their honor, their conscience, their ideal, or however else we may please to distinguish it.

The belief in a transcendental God, from lack of clearer ideas, long served our forefathers to symbolize this immanent God. Therefore we will not vilify the old views; they after all contain a great truth. We shall treat them with reverence, notwithstanding we reject them. To us the idea of a God, absolutely existing, has become a superstition; but all the more have we thus come to know the meaning of the God we have abstracted from the reality of the world and from the life of our heart. In this sense, the Faust of Goethe speaks:

> "The God that in my breast is owned
> Can deeply stir the inward sources,
> The God above my powers enthroned
> He cannot change external forces."

The idea of a transmundane God, a God of itself, would be an attempt to create 'a noumenon in the positive sense,' (as Kant calls it) which is inadmissible. There is no reality corresponding to it. However, the idea of a God as the possible presence of a moral law in the world to which we have to conform, is a conception of pure thought which involves no self-contradiction. It would be (to use Kant's expression again) 'a noumenon in the negative sense,' the use of which is admissible and even indispensable for arriving at general conceptions. The idea of God in this sense, it will be found, has some realities corresponding to it, just as much as the quality of heaviness or weight corresponds to our conception of gravity. The God outside of the world is an anthropomorphism, and is as such a remnant of former ages. Monism leads us to the purer and loftier idea of an immanent God. Goethe says:

> " What were a God who from the outside stirred
> So that the world around his finger whirred?
> He from within the Universe must move,
> Nature in Him and Him in nature prove.
> Thus all that in him lives and moves and is
> Will ne'er his power and his spirit miss."

Agnosticism believes that the substance of these spirits, things absolute, as well as their existence, is an inscrutable mystery of which we can know nothing. Monism goes a step beyond this. According to Monism, the division of the world into knowable things, as appearing in their operations, and into absolutely unknowable things held to exist behind or in phenomena, is an untenable and self-contradictory dualism. Monism rejects altogether the ghost-illusion of existence absolute, and constantly keeps in mind that every thing is a part only of the All, and that every natural process is only an aspect of the entire indivisible existence of the universe. We, too, are a part of the eternal All in which we live, move, and have our being.

THE STRONGHOLD OF MYSTICISM.

I.

THE UNKNOWABLE.

THE most modern specter that haunts the realms of philosophy goes under the name of the Unknowable. Ghosts and goblins are done away with by science, but, in spite of that, superstition returns and assumes a vaguer and more indistinct form in the idea of an indefinite and undefinable something which is supposed to be an inscrutable mystery. Some people fear it as a hidden power, some reverence it as the embodiment of perfection, some love it as a fit object of their unaccountable longings, and almost all who in their fantastical visions imagine to conceive it, bow down and worship it. It is the Baal of modern philosophy, and even the iconoclasts of the nineteenth century have not freed themselves from this fetish. While denouncing supernaturalism in the religious creeds of to-day, they preach the supernaturalism of a mystic Unknowable that lies beyond human experience, and do not seem to be aware of their inconsistency.

The Unknowable is like the fog which the Anglo-Saxon saga relates was rising in the shape of the giant Grendel from the fens and marshes in Jutland, and "haunted the halls of men." It is an intangible monster that hides the real aspect of things from the human eye and spreads an unwholesome mysticism about all our conceptions.

The world, however, does not consist of things recognizable, and of fog around or within them. Natural phenomena do not emanate from transcendent sources. Nature is one throughout, and natural phenomena are linked together by causation. Causality, the law of causation, is not a capricious ukase of an autocratic demiurge, who, like a human monarch, rules the world according to the maxim, *car tel est notre bon plaisir*. Causation is no mysterious process ; its law is demonstrable and explainable. In accordance with the conservation of matter and energy, causality signifies the identity of matter and energy in a change of form. Fundamentally, causality rests on the same evidence as the logical rule of indentity, and is in its most general aspect as simple as the arithmetical formula " once one is one."

The idea of the Unknowable has its root in the relativity of knowledge. We know things only by the way they affect us. Subjective sensations are the elements of all objective knowledge. Knowledge being itself a relation, the agnostic should but try to state in clear terms what he conceives 'absolute knowledge' to be, and his unattainable ideal of 'absolute knowledge' will explode in the attempt.

Every manifestation of nature that affects us either directly or indirectly can thus afford us material for our sensation. Inasmuch as all existence must manifest its existence somehow (if it did not, it could not be said to exist), we maintain that all existence can at least indirectly be or become an object of cognition.

The existence of a thing implies the manifestation of its existence. It exists only in so far as it manifests itself, and every manifestation, producing somehow an effect either directly on ourselves or indirectly on other things can be (directly or indirectly) observed, described, inquired into, and comprehended. Absolute existence which is not manifested in some way means non-existence, it is a *contradictio in adjecto* and a chimerical impossibility. Hegel says : " Existence and non-existence are identical." This is true if Hegel refers to an absolute existence, or an existence in and of itself.

The unknown is by no means unknowable, for our ignorance of some subject does not justify the dogmatic assertion, that it can not be known at all. There are many problems which have not yet been investigated, and there are innumerable things we do not yet know of, but there are no phenomena in the world which *per se* are unintelligible. The vastness and grandeur of the world are so great that the province of science is unlimited, and after each discovery new problems will constantly present themselves to keep the inquiring scientists busy. The new problems will be born from the very explanations of the old problems, and they will open new vistas of research of which we never before dreamed of ; but wherever our inquiring mind may venture, we shall find that, throughout, nature is intelligible.

Nature is not mysterious ; if it appears to us mysterious, it is a proof of our ignorance and of our misconception of nature. The mystery lies in the subject not in the object; and we should always endeavor to formulate it in an intelligent question. A thoughtful mind is not overawed by things which he does not understand, but he treats them as problems and tries to solve them.

Nature, it is true, is wonderful ; but what is most wonderful is that the most intricate and complicated phenomena of Nature are marvelously simple in their ultimate and elementary conditions.

II.

THE FASHIONABLE MYSTICISM OF TO-DAY

THERE are many philosophers—or so-called philosophers—whose avowed object it is to introduce us into the mysteries of the absolute. A philosophy that as a matter of principle takes its stand on the data of positive science aims at nothing of the kind ; it sees the main object of philosophy in clearing away the fogs of mysticism, and from this standpoint we attempt to present definite solutions of the fundamental problems in clear and popular language.

While pressing this anti-mystical tendency the author of these essays feels in duty bound to express his esteem for the mysticism of the fourteenth century as represented in Master Eckhart of Augsburg, and Johannes Tauler of Strassburg. The historian recognizes in this powerful and enthusiastic movement the preparation and beginning of the Reformation. But it was more than that ; it was a religious movement which dimly foreshadowed the future Religion of Monism, *i. e.,* a faith by which the individual would find salvation and comfort in his oneness with the All. The idea of resigning all egotism and becoming God-like by oneness with the All, was drawn from the living well of man's religious sentiment, and it was justified by the New Testament. This idea was the quintessence of Eckhart's and Tauler's doctrines, which in those days could be grasped and presented, could rise in the Church with the Pope's approval, and become popular with the masses, only in the garb of mysticism.

The mysticism of Eckhart and Tauler (if we exclude the narrowness of certain views that belonged to their time rather than to their ideal) is very different from the fashionable mysticism of to-day. The secret which they were revealing, like the moral instructions of Christ, had an ethical importance; it appeared as a mystery only to the worldling whose spiritual eye is closed. But it was no absolute mystery; it was a clear and plain truth to the knowing. Like the moral maxims of primitive Christianity, it could and it should become a truism universally acknowledged and accepted. Christ said: "What I tell you in darkness that speak ye in the light; and what ye hear in the ear, that preach ye upon the housetops."

The fashionable mysticism of the day is a lack of intellectual grasp and laziness of thought. The old mysticism arose from a fulness of the heart; a moral truth was recognized which seemed to conflict with wisdom and perhaps conflicted indeed with worldly prudence. The mystic of to-day takes the unsolved problem as inscrutable and thus by limiting his mind easily settles his doubts; the religious mystics found in the abyss of man's bosom the self-same power at work that bears and sustains the whole universe; the *ego* was recognized as a transient phenomenon of the everlasting All, and if man desires to live, he must (to use Tauler's expression) surrender his *ego* and become God (*entwerden um Gott zu werden*). They were mystics because they preached the paradox to gain all things through self-denial, and to become All by doffing that which seemed to be our individual self, and to live by abandoning the passions that grow from the properly egotistic existence.

Let us not worship the unknown, but let us declare war against it ; let us conquer it. If there is any maxim in science and philosophy that can be justified, it is this : there is nothing unknowable ; no problem is *per se* insolvable. A philosopher whose philosophy ends in something unknowable may be compared to a man working out a computation which does not come out right.

A problem that is not solvable but insearchable, is no problem, but unmitigated nonsense. If it has sense, it must be solvable, although with our current knowledge and with insufficient methods of investigation *we* at present may not be able to solve it. It is, then, unsolved, but not insolvable.

*   *   *

THE irrational in mathematics might be paraded as an analogy to Mr. Spencer's idea of the Unknowable. But the irrational is a very inappropriate expression for a process that on the contrary is purely and exclusively rational but imaginary. To extract the root of -1 ($\sqrt{-1}$) cannot be realized and the irrational would properly be called the unrealizable.

The infinite is another conception that being misunderstood by unmathematical minds serves as a basis of mysticism.

III.

THE INFINITE A MATHEMATICAL TERM.

IN the realm of mysteries the infinite is monarch. Even those who have freed themselves from the belief

in 'things of themselves,' in transcendent forces, and
absolute entities, are, as a rule, faithful worshipers at
the shrine of the mystery of mysteries. Here they
think the limit of human reason is reached, here we
have to bow in silent adoration.

The Infinite, however, and its correlative, the Eternal, are as little mysterious as any other of our abstract
ideas. There is no reason for spelling it with a capital I, or for making it an object of religious sentiment.
If we do not understand the origin, purpose, and meaning of these conceptions, we had better go to work and
study them. Man is given dominion over the whole
creation and not the least part of the creation is the
intellectual world of man's own ideas. However, in
order to have dominion over it, man must by worthy
of it. He must conquer it.

The infinite is a symbol for a mathematical process. When I count I may count up to a hundred or
two hundred, to a thousand or to a million, or to whatever number I please. If I do not stop for other reasons, I may count on without stopping—in a word,
into infinity.

Infinitude is never an accomplished process. Take
for instance an infinite decimal, say a recurring decimal. It is a decimal fraction which we think of
without a limit. Thus $\frac{1}{3} = 0.3333\ldots$ The dots
indicate that the process of placing threes in the decimal fraction can be carried on *ad infinitum.* The
more threes are put there, the nearer will the decimal
be equal to $\frac{1}{3}$. It will never be absolutely equal and
we may stop short as soon as the error resulting from
it becomes immaterial.

We can produce an infinitude wherever we can
apply such an infinite process. If we soar into the

heavens and let our thoughts wander into cosmic space, we may proceed from star to star in the milky way and beyond we may perhaps reach other milky ways. If we still proceed we may wander in empty space for ever and ever. If these wanderings were possible we need as little stop as in counting.

A drop of mercury can just as well be used as an instance of infinitude as the universe. It can be divided into two halves, and each half is again divisible. It is divisible *ad infinitum* because the division is a process which may be carried on as long as one pleases. The infinitely small is no more a thing in itself than the infinitely great, and there is no more mystery in the one than in the other.

IV.

IS THE INFINITE MYSTERIOUS.

Mr. L. T. Ives presents to the elimination of the mysterious in our conception of infinitude the following objection :*

"When the word infinity is used, a something is expressed that cannot be made or reached by addition. In this respect it is certainly unlike anything with which we have had experience. The immense distances dealt with in astronomy, are, by simply enlarging our unit of measurement, as readily disposed of as measuring thirty-six inches of ribbon, and by a similar process. But when we come to something which no enlargement of our unit will affect, something to which the diameter of our sidereal system would be as a unit of measurement no better than the diameter of a sand grain, then surely we have reached a something not a symbol of anything save itself, and about which it cannot truly be said, 'there is no mystery.'

*The Open Court, p. 872

" Does not infinite space present this problem ?   You say, 'beyond nature is empty non-existence.'   This empty non-existence is infinite room for existence, infinite space—space without limit.   We say 'without limit' because we cannot conceive it as having limit.   The space we know here is not empty, so, judging from experience, there is reason to believe infinite space not empty —and the problem that presents itself to our thought is infinite fullness rather than infinite emptiness.   But in either case the infinite element remains the same."

The fundamental error in this statement is that infinity is from the beginning supposed to be *something*. People hearing infinitude spoken of in solemn terms suppose that the process is realized in nature somewhere ; when asked to conceive the infinite théy are overawed by the thought that they are themselves unable to accomplish the task.   They believe that the infinite is a real entity, and in the vain attempt to grasp it despair at last of ever reaching the end of the infinite.

*   *   *

BUT is not the space of the world truly an infinitude that is realized in actual existence ?

The method of solving the problem has been indicated by no less a man than the great sage of Königsberg, by Immanuel Kant.   Before entering into a discussion of the infinitude of Space and the eternity of Time, we must have a clear conception as to the nature of Space and Time.   We do not agree with Kant, but we adopt his method and attempt to solve the problem in the way it is presented in the Critique of Pure Reason.

V.

SPACE AND TIME.

In his Critique of Pure Reason (Part I, Section I), Kant proposes the question : " What then are time and space ? Are they real existences ?" And he answers in the negative. He says :

"If we ascribe objective reality to these forms of representation, it becomes impossible to avoid changing every thing into mere appearance. For if we regard space and time as properties, which must be found in objects as things in themselves, as *sine quibus non* of the possibility of their existence, and reflect on the absurdities in which we then find ourselves involved, inasmuch as we are compelled to admit the existence of two infinite things, which are nevertheless not substances, nor any thing really inhering in substances, nay, to admit that they are the necessary conditions of the existence of all things, and moreover, that they must continue to exist, although all existing things were annihilated, — we cannot blame the good Berkeley for degrading bodies to mere illusory appearances. Nay, even our own existence, which would in this case depend upon the self-existent reality of such a mere nonentity as time, would necessarily be changed with it into mere appearance—an absurdity which no one has as yet been guilty of."

Space and time, Kant declares, are nothing else than forms, the one of our external the other of our internal sense. They are not real, they are ideal.

We agree with Kant that space and time are ideal, not real in so far as they are no things, no objects, but abstract conceptions. Space of itself apart from extended, extending or moving things, and time of itself apart from changes do as little exist as matter of itself or force of itself. Space does not extend, but things extend and move ; and their extension *is* space. Time does not change but things are changing ; their change,

or rather the measure of their change, *is* time.   Without extended things no space, and without motion or
change no time.   We disagree from Kant in so far as
he says that space and time are the forms *of the thinking subject only.*   He denies that they are properties
inhering in the objects, because, he maintains, they
cannot have been abstracted from reality.   If they
were abstracted from reality, he argues, mathematics
would be an experimental, yet no transcendental, *i. e.*
formal, science, and we could never attribute to mathematics absolute validity (rigid necessity and universality).   Kant explains his position as follows :

  "Those who maintain the absolute reality of time and space,
whether as essentially subsisting, or only inhering, as modifications,
in things, must find themselves at utter variance with the principles of experience itself.   For, if they decide for the first view,
and make space and time into substances, this being the side taken
by mathematical natural philosophers, they must admit two self-
subsisting nonentities, infinite and eternal, which exist (yet without
there being any thing real) for the purpose of containing in themselves every thing that is real.

  "If they adopt the second view of inherence, which is pre-
ferred by some metaphysical natural philosophers, and regard
space and time as relations (contiguity in space or succession in
time), abstracted from experience, though represented confusedly
in this state of separation, they find themselves in that case neces-
sitated to deny the validity of mathematical doctrines *a priori* in
reference to real things (for example, in space),—at all events their
apodeictic certainty.   For such certainty cannot be found in an
a posteriori proposition ; and the conceptions *a priori* of space and
time are, according to this opinion, mere creations of the imagination, having their source really in experience."

From this standpoint Kant concludes :

  "I maintain that the properties of space and time, in conformity to which I set both, as the condition of their existence,
abide in my mode of intuition, and not in the objects in themselves."

Taking this position that space and time are forms of our cognition merely, not of things, Kant accepts the inevitable consequence that

"The question, 'What are objects considered as things in themselves ?,' remains unanswerable even after the most thorough examination of the phenomenal world."

If Kant were right in his solution of the problem, the question "How does the constitution of thinking subjects universally, (so far as we can judge), happen to have such forms of space and time as they are," would be unanswerable. Could we not, or at least some of us—of living beings—just as well have a constitution of four-dimensional space? And if so, how would in that case our conception of four dimensional space tally with actual space?

If space inhered, as Kant maintains, in the thinking subject *only*, special relations and laws would appear different to four-dimensional beings. Kepler's third law for instance, that "the squares of the times of revolution of the planets are always proportional to the cubes of their mean distances from the sun," would to them most probably appear as "the cubes of their times of revolution being proportional to their mean distances taken to the fourth power." To us a right-angled solid that measures two inches in each of its dimensions, (*viz.*, a cube) contains eight cubic inches. A four-dimensional being would be sure that a right-angled solid that measures in all its dimensions two inches must necessarily contain sixteen four-dimensional inches. Anybody who denies that such radical changes would take place in the objects of the phenomenal world, must inevitably admit that tridimensionality is not merely our "mode of intuition," but an inherent quality of matter.

If the form of matter is tridimensional it is natural that beings whose bodies are built up of tridimensional matter will be able to ascertain the tridimensionality of their world by experiments of mere inner experience. Taking up space themselves. they can by mere reflexion determine how many dimensions actually exist. Kant does not distinguish such internal experimenting from reasoning a priori. Reasoning a priori should be strictly limited to pure formal thought, while experiments are and remain a matter of experience whether they are executed on phenomena of the outer world or whether the subject experiments on or within his own body, which after all, like the rest of things, is an object in the phenomenal world.

If Kant had investigated the problem of the a priori (of formal thought), he would have found that the forms of our cognition naturally grow with experience, and that we acquire them indeed by abstraction. Consequently, absolute apriority which Kant attributes to space can not be granted it. Our mathematical laws possess absolute rigidity and universality for tridimensional space and as a system of third degree they are a priori, *i. e.*, pure formal thought, but the fact that space is tridimentional is exclusively a matter of experience.

How much of experience enters into our conception of space can be seen from the following logical syllogism :

PREMISSA MAJOR :

The formal laws of a system of third degree apply to any system of third degree with rigidity and universality, as we know a priori (*i. e.*, from pure reason, or formal thought, from inner reflection upon the laws of pure form).

PREMISSA MINOR :

Actual space being tridimensional is a system of third degree,
as we know by experience and can prove by experiment.

ERGO:

The formal laws of third degree apply to space with rigidity and universality.

* * *

KANT, in his argument, identifies 'ideal' and 'subjective.' The conception of space being an abstract idea and its being to some extent formal thought, does by no means compel us to deny that actual space is a real (although by no means a material) property in objects.

Kant says:

"The proposition, "All objects are beside each other in space," is valid only under the limitation that these things are taken as objects of *our sensuous intuition.* But if I join the condition to the conception, and say, 'all things, as external *phenomena,* are beside each other in space,' then the rule is valid universally, and without any limitation.

"Our expositions, consequently, teach the *reality* (*i. e.* the objective validity) of space in regard of all phenomena which can be presented to us externally as objects, and at the same time also the *ideality* of space in regard to objects when they are considered by means of reason as things in themselves, that is, without reference to the constitution of our sensibility. We maintain, therefore, the *empirical ideality* of space in regard to all possible external experience although we must admit its *transcendental ideality,* in other words, that it is nothing, so soon as we withdraw the condition upon which the possibility of all experience depends, and look upon space as something that belongs to things in themselves."

Whether space and time apply to "things in themselves"-must be considered from the standpoint of monism as an idle question, since "things in themselves" do not exist.

In contradistinction to Kant's view we maintain: The nature of our cognition is such that space can not but appear tridimensional to us. Our existence is tridimensional, and for that very reason our cognition is tridimensional also. Our existence, however, is a part of the whole of reality and our life is a phenomenon among many other innumerable processes of nature. Consequently we look upon the forms of our existence as upon a specimen, so to speak, of the forms of existence in general.

It does not lie within the scope of our problem to enter into the details of the growth of space-conception. There is but one way for a living being to acquire the idea of space, and that is by motion—not only through the observation of moving bodies, but also and chiefly through self-motion. If we were immovably fixed to one spot, we would have no conception of space or at least a very dim one. Only while moving ourselves, can we measure distances, and by measuring we form our ideas about space. If this is true, and I think it can be proved experimentally, the definition of space as "the possibility of motion in all directions" will be justified. That the different senses having a different kind of motion, will have different measures for space is obvious. The most primitive method of the different senses in judging of distances is the remembrance of the effort necessary to pass through it from one end to the other. Errors are corrected by a comparison among the results of the different senses and may be altogether avoided by the application of a standard measure in which all distances can be expressed.

VI.

INFINITUDE AND ETERNITY.

THE problem of Infinitude and Eternity depends upon a correct view of space and time. "Space in and of itself—apart from reality—does not exist, save in our imagination. Space is abstracted from reality. We abstract extension, *i. e.*, the relational, and omit all material. Hegel defines space as *Das Neben-einander der Dinge* (The beside-another of things). But space is more than actual relation and extension, it is also the possibility of new relation and further extension. Accordingly we prefer to call it the possible direction of motion. If space is any possible direction of a point* or a particle of matter, there can be no doubt as to the infinitude of space ; for the possibility of motion is infinite in every direction. This fact is thus self-evident from the definition of space.

If we think of space as a real entity, it is the greatest mystery—a mystery which, we must confess, can never be solved. If we recognize that space is a symbol for a possibility, *i. e.*, for an unlimited process, everything is clear, and there is just as little mystery in the infinitude of space as in the infinitude of a recurring decimal like 0.333. . . . .

The only correct usage of the word 'infinite' is that

---

* A posited point is no real existence, but it presupposes a positing being, which in order to exist must be a material reality.

of the mathematical term. As a poetic license, however, we use it also in the sense of 'immeasurable.' We speak of the infinite ocean and the infinite depth of the sea, although both are very definite and even not immeasurable. So also the "infinite" world, the universe, is a definite reality. Certainly it is in its totality immeasurable; but we recognize that its energy as well as its matter can neither increase nor decrease, a fact which is now indorsed by science and generally styled the law of conservation of matter and energy.

As of space, the same thing holds good of time. Time is also an abstract; absolute time does not exist. Schopenhauer is right in saying that neither past nor future exist ; the only real time is the present and it *is* always.

Time is a generalization or abstract of existence in regard to its continuance or possible change, but without reference to anything else, be it matter or form. Hegel calls it *Das Nach-ein-ander der Dinge* (the after-another of things). This can lead to a misconception if by "things" in their totality we mean the world. The material things in their totality *are* always; they exist not one after another, but are simultaneous and thus matter remains in all changes permanent. To express it in two words : *Reality is,* which *is* includes that it has existed and that it is going to exist. Hegel's definition, however, is correct in so far as things are considered as changeable forms. It is motion which changes things either in their mutual relation, or their forms. Time, accordingly, can only be measured by motion ; and, indeed, time is the 'measure of motion' and nothing more.*

---

* Aristotle uses an unfortunate expression when defining time as the number of motion ὁ χρόνος ἀριθμός ἐστι κινήσεως.

If time is conceived as an objectively existing entity, we will soon find out that it is inconceivable and full of self-contradiction. It would be the realization of an unlimited process, the actualization of an impossibility, and the bold establishment of a palpable self-contradiction. Kant justly maintains that objective time (just as much as objective space) is an absurdity.

Past and Future are still more complicated abstracts than the present. When conceiving them as objective existences, we are driven to statements which are inconceivable and impossible. They are without limit. Infinitude in time is called eternity. Eternity, conceived as a real thing, is a self-contradiction.

The decimal 0.333 . . . is not a finished magnitude; it is a process to approximate ⅓, but it is never equal to ⅓. If we should demand that an infinite decimal like 0.3333 . . . . be complete, and equal to ⅓, we would be made to understand that this demand is absurd and its realization impossible. We cannot finish it and cannot even conceive of an infinite decimal as being finished. But we use where it is wanted the cipher 0.333 . . . for indicating or symbolizing it. The words ' Past ' and ' Future ' are in no less a degree symbols of a process that does not admit of a full realization.

The eternity of the Past is an unlimited retrogressive motion. It attempts to comprehend in one conception all the changes which we can imagine to have anteceded the state of reality as it is now. The eternity of the future is the infinite and indefinite possibility of the changes to come after the present state of things. And thus both are fundamentally an eternity of the present time, which means that time must be conceived as limitless. Reality existed always and will exist always, and the possibility of change cannot be exhausted—at least we can imagine it to be inexhaustible, or if exhaustible we can imagine that certain long series of changes can periodically be repeated over and over again.

Time is an abstract from Reality. Reality by all its changes remains. Past, Present, and Future are abstracts of the states of Reality, with respect to whether they are, or have been, or are going to be.

This form of expression 'are, have been, or are going to be,' is most correct for our present purpose, as it defines both past as well as future in the present tenses 'they *have*' and 'they *are* going to be.' The present only is real ; both past as well as future must thus be conceived as special aspects of the present.

Space and time, infinitude and eternity, are no mysteries unless we make them such by wrongly attributing to them a 'thingish' or objective reality which they do not possess.

The nations of old worshiped Space and Time, Infinitude and Eternity, and we now smile at their errors and call them pagans. It is a paganism superior to fetishism, as its idol is woven out of the most delicate woof which can be obtained, *viz.*: the ideas of the thinker. But there is no essential difference between this higher kind of paganism and fetishism ; it is a difference of degree.

Kronos and his colleagues belong to the past, but the worship of eternity and infinitude still obtains with our present generation, and will continue to be an object of idolatry until we understand that infinitude and eternity are creations of ourown minds.

AGNOSTICISM AND POSITIVISM

THE positive philosophy of Auguste Comte has
been most severely attacked in England by those who
should have hailed the French thinker as their best
ally and co-worker, by Mr. J. S. Mill, Mr. Herbert
Spencer and Professor Huxley. And yet all three are
inspired, like Mr. Comte, with an arduous and holy
zeal to free the human mind from traditional dogmatism ; all three have devoted their lives to establish a
new philosophy of radical free thought. But what is
stranger still, all three,. especially Mr. Spencer and
Prof. Huxley, are entangled in the very same error as
their great French predecessor. They all together believe in the unknowability of absolute existence, of
the unconditioned, of that which lies beyond phenomena, and thus failed in their aspirations to present a
philosophy of positive science. They did not succeed
in liberating us from mysticism. They all are Agnostics.

M. Comte observes* that there are three phases of
intellectual evolution, for the individual as well as for
the mass : the *Theological* (or *Supernatural*), the *Metaphysical* and the *Positive.*

In the theological phase the mind explains phenomena in a mythological way as the productions of
supernatural agents. In the metaphysical phase the

* Compare "Comte's Philosophy of the Sciences," by G. H. Lewes, pp.
10, 11, and 18.

supernatural agents are set aside for abstract forces and entities. In the positive phase the mind, convinced of the futility of all enquiry into causes and essences, restricts itself to the observation and classification of phenomena, and to the discovery of the invariable relations of succession and similitude which things bear to each other : in a word, to the discovery of the laws of phenomena. "The metaphysician," M. Comte says, "believes he can penetrate into the causes and essences of the phenomena around him, while the positivist recognizes his incompetency and limits his efforts to the ascertainment of the laws which regulate the succession of these phenomena."

Between the second and third phase, according to M. Comte's definition, there is no other essential difference than the "conviction of the futility of all enquiry into causes and essences." And this conviction is the main doctrine of agnosticism. M. Comte accordingly was truly an agnostic before Prof. Huxley invented the term, and before Mr. Spencer wrote his First Principles. All the difference between M. Comte on the one hand and agnostic thinkers on the other are of secondary importance. They are like sectarian divergencies among denominations of the same creed.

We consider as M. August Comte's greatest merit —aside from his ardent enthusiasm for truth in philosophic enquiry, and for reform in our state of society—the invention of the term "positive " which is a very expressive word. But we do not understand by "positive," as does M. Comte, any limitation of the human mind. We understand by " positive " the monistic view of a unitary conception of the world.

Positivism, as we should express ourselves, recognizes that the so-called phenomena are positive facts, that there are neither causes nor essences behind them, that Absolute Existence or the Unconditioned, or the Metaphisical (or by whatever name the Unknowable may be called) are chimerical nonentities, self-contradictory conceptions, and impossibilities.

By experience only man becomes familiar with the facts of existence. The facts of existence are no phenomenal sham; they are real, and knowledge means the systematical arrangement of experiences.

M. Comte erroneously considered Kant as the representative metaphysical philosopher. In truth it was Kant who struck the first vigorous blow at the errors of ontology and the belief in absolute existence, while M. Comte was still as deep entangled in metaphysicism as are his English rivals and opponents, the partisans of agnosticism.

We are little helped if we are told that we can never know anything about the causes and essences of things and that the Unconditioned is an inaccessible province which we should not attempt to enter. This view which is so excellently and adequately called agnosticism, appears from our conception of positivism, as a transition from the metaphysical to a truly positive phase. It is the last remnant of dualism. In the philosophical conception of agnosticism, the metaphysical essences have faded into vague unknowabilities and will disappear entirely as soon as the idea of absolute existence is recognized as untenable ground— as soon as philosophy is conceived as a unitary conception of the facts of reality.

IDEALISM AND REALISM.

THE old opposition between Idealism and Realism has, from the standpoint of monism, become immaterial. Both are right in their way, and, in so far as they are severally insufficient, both are wrong.

Idealism starts from thought and sensation, from the subjective aspect of phenomena, and in its most consistent form, as spiritualism, denies the existence of matter. Realism starts from real existence, from the objective aspect of phenomena, and in its most consistent form, as materialism, denies the existence of spirit.

Now, as a matter of fact, neither spirit nor matter exist of themselves: they are abstracts. Realism is right in so far as the facts of reality cannot be considered as sham. Idealism, on the other hand, is also right, in as far as the building-stones of all knowledge are our sensations; they are the facts of reality. However, the processes that within our body produce the subjective feeling of sensations, can not be considered as essentially different from the phenomena of the outer world; since science, the classified system of observations, shows that the former not only are most intimately interwoven with and conditioned by the latter, but that they must have grown from them in the process of natural evolution.

Idealism pretends that sensations are radically different from the phenomena perceived. The sensation of light is different from ether-waves, the sensation of sound different from the vibrations of the air. In his excellent essay, " Sensation and the Outer World," M. Alfred Binet says :

" Suppose that, my eyes being closed, I lay my hand upon my table, and that I feel a pin rolling about beneath my finger ; I experience a sensation of a tactile kind, which excites in me a series of inferences, conscious, sub-conscious, and unconscious, and the whole occurrence is comprised in the following judgment: I touch a pin. In this way, through external perception, we possess knowledge of objects by the sensations they produce in us. * * *

" That which has produced our sensation of a pin, is not *directly* the pin ; it is the nervous modification which that object has produced, in acting upon our sense of touch ; our sensation follows this nervous modification. * * *

" Nothing resembles less the external object than the excitation it propagates in our nervous substance. What resemblance is there, for example, between the head of a pin that lies beneath my finger, and the physico-chemical phenomenon that passes through the sensitive fibers of my hand and that reaches my brain through the spinal marrow, where it gives rise to the conscious perception of a pin. Plainly, here are phenomena entirely dissimilar. It follows, therefore, that if there is a fact, at the present day, firmly established, it is that the sensations we experience upon contact with external objects are in no particular the copy of those objects. There is nothing outside of my eye that is like color or light, nothing outside of my organ of hearing that is like noise or sound, nothing outside of my sense of touch that is like hardness or softness or resistance, nothing outside of my sense of smell that is like a perfume, nothing apart from my sense of taste that is like a flavor." * * *

Sensation and the phenomena of the outer world are different. Sensations are not the real copies or images proper of things. The nervous system is not actually a mirror to reflect phenomena just as they are. Yet we may justly compare it to a mirror. For, after all, certain features of the phenomena are preserved. They are consequently not so entirely different as is maintained. A certain form of a phenomenon corresponds to a certain form of sensation. The phenomena being different among themselves produce sensations that in their turn also are different among themselves. And the difference suffices to distinguish them.

The electric current in the wire of a telephone is entirely different from the air-waves of sound. Nevertheless the form of air-waves produced by spoken words can be translated, as it were, into the electric current and from the electric current back again into air-waves. Both can adapt themselves to the same form and thus become messengers of information. Must we declare that all communication through the telephone is impossible because electricity and sound-waves, wire and air, are entirely different?

It is true that the pin on the table does not resemble the physico-chemical phenomenon that takes place in our nerves. But it is true nevertheless that this physico-chemical phenomenon of our sensation together with the memories of other sensations, especially those of touch and sight, produces in our mind the conception of a pin. In spite of all difference between the outer world and sensation, the pin as we conceive it to be, is the net result of such sensations. This is possible as in the example of the telephone by a transference of motion from one medium to another through the *preservation of form.* The same is true of the whole world. Our conception of the world, in order to be true, must ultimately be based on the facts of sensation—not on the subjective aspect of sensation only, but also and especially on its objective aspect as motions of a special form. In this way only can we acquire a conception of the objects, as they must be supposed to be independent of the subject.

The difference between the phenomena of the outer world and sensations, appears more striking than it really is, because, in order to understand a process fully, we must reduce it to some form which can be expressed in mathematical symbols or figures. Formal thought is always the basis of a scientific comprehension, and in order to comprehend a phenomenon, so as to measure and calculate it, we must in many cases translate it, as it were, into the language of that sense which is the organ of measurement and calculation. Therefore audible sound-phenomena are represented as visible air-waves. Hence the growing importance of the sense of sight.

Cognition never alters the data of sensory experience, although the invention of instruments may enlarge its reach. The Copernican system differs from the naïve view, that the earth is a flat disk, not because it denies or contradicts the facts of sensation, but because it arranges them more systematically with the assistance of mathematics (*i. e.* the method of formal thought).

It is a misconception of knowledge to demand that it should be something different than a methodical arrangement of facts. Our cognition, although it may translate one sensation into another, never indeed goes, nor need it go, beyond sensation.

*   *   *

BUT if cognition is merely the arrangement of the data of sense-perception, if the thinking subject cannot go beyond his sensations, are we not indeed limited to the subjective aspect of phenomena and does not their objective aspect remain to us a book with seven seals?

This objection is made, indeed and that too, by most subtle thinkers; it is based upon a deep insight into the nature of cognition; but it is nevertheless erroneous, because it overlooks one most important point. The subjective aspect of sensation which we call feeling, and the objective aspect of sensation which is a physiological phenomenon, and as such a process of motion, are actually one and the same thing. They are two aspects only of one and the same indivisible fact.

Professor Bunge, of Basel, says in his pamphlet "Vitalism and Mechanism" :*

"True, the eye is a physical apparatus, an optical mechanism, a camera obscura. The image on the retina is produced at the back of the eye, in conformity with the same immutable laws of refraction that regulate the production of an image on the photographer's plate. But—surely that is no psychical phenomenon. The eye plays purely a passive part in that operation. The retinal image, moreover, may be produced in an eye that has been removed from its socket—in a dead eye.

"The *evolution* of the eye—that is a psychical phenomenon! How has this complicated optical apparatus been formed? Why do the cells of the tissues so unite with one another as to produce this wonderful structure? That is the great problem, to the solution of which the first step has not as yet been taken. Undoubtedly, the *succesion* in which the evolutionary processes have taken place, admit of observation and description ; but of the *reasons* we know absolutely nothing. * * *

"All processes in our organisms, I maintain, that admit of mechanical explanation, are just as little psychical phenomena as the movements of the leaves and the branches on a tree, shaken by the blasts of a storm. * * *

"In *activity* lies hidden the mystery of life. The notion of

* Leipsic : F. C. W. Vogel.

activity, however, has not been derived from sensory perception, but from *self-observation*—from the observation of the will, as it strikes our consciousness, as it is revealed to the *inward* sense. And when this self-same thing meets the outward senses, we do not again recognize it. We see perfectly well what it does and what is done to it—mechanical processes. But the pith of the matter we cannot get at." * * *

Professor Bunge contradicts himself when stating that we know absolutely nothing of the reasons. He says in another passage of the same pamphlet :

" Our cognition must proceed from the known of our inner world to the unknown of the outer world."

We can indeed get at the pith of the matter. The solution of the problem as to the "activity " of life is contained in another sentence of Professor Bunge that follows in the very same paragraph. He says :

"If this self-same thing meets the outward senses, we do not again recognize it."

That mysterious activity in the outer world, that kernel within, which is supposed to be unknowable, is the self-same thing that we ourselves are.

And Schopenhauer, the admirer of Hindoo philosophy, is correct in so far as he says that we can indeed look behind the veil of Maya, not in natural phenomena, but in ourselves. The phenomenon of our existence, he says, is our body in all its knowable relations and manifestations, the kernel is that something which Schopenhauer calls ' Will.'

However, this something (the Will of Schopenhauer) can be analyzed, and is found to be of a very complicated nature which grows in a process of evolution from the simplest conditions to more and more complicated combinations. While analyzing it, we experience that the kernel supposed to be behind its phenomenal manifestation is inseparably connected with it—yea, it is identical with it.

Now, in analyzing the phenomena of nature we apprehend them as manifestations, the motions of which can be mechanically traced. If their motions are not actually explained, they are at least explainable. The residuum which is left is the spontaneity that pervades all processes of nature. Nature is not passive, it is no dead machine acted upon from the outside by push. Its manifestations must be considered as active processes of self-motion.

This conception of nature is corroborated by the fact that the psychical and physiological life of organisms must have developed from non-organized substances. The phenomena of non-organized nature, accordingly must contain the conditions and possibilities of all higher organized life.

Thus the objective aspect of sensation, which is a phenomenon of motion, is, at least in theory, mechanically explainable. Not so the subjective aspect of sensation, which we designate as feeling that accompanies the process. Feeling (in so far as we understand by the word the psychical phenomenon only, and not its physiological basis) being no motion, it would be absurd to look for a mechanical explanation of feeling in this sense.

The motion of every muscle and nerve is determined so that it might be expressed in definite figures, but the subjective aspect, alone and by itself, to the exclusion of its objective manifestations, cannot be expressed in mathematical terms. In order to know what this "activity," the spontaneity of willing and perceiving, is, we must experience it ourselves.

We can measure the intensity and duration of feeling in its objective aspect as a motion, but its subjective aspect can only be felt. The mental feeling is, so to say, the inseparable 'within' of the physiological phenomenon, which corresponds to the emotion. The note *C major* can be mathematically explained as a special form of motion in our auditory nerve; but the living feeling that apprehends it as a sound, can not; it is nevertheless a fact of experience; and there is no other possibility than to consider them both as one: —as two aspects of one reality.

* * *

In the old quarrels of the schools, idealism in its extreme form had one great advantage over materialism. It took its stand on the given facts of sensation. Thus it could not be refuted on its own grounds. Baron Holbach says:

"What shall we say of Berkley who endeavors to prove that everything in the world is a chimerical illusion and that the universe exists only in ourselves and in our imagination. He makes the existence of all things doubtful by means of *sophisms which are unanswerable* to those who accept the spirituality of the soul."

In a similar way Lord Byron acknowledged the validity of Berkley's arguments. He said:*

" When Bishop Berkeley said 'there was no matter,'
And proved it—'twas no matter what he said.
They say his system 'tis in vain to batter,
Too subtle for the airiest human head,
And yet who can believe it? I would shatter
Gladly all matters down to stone and lead.
Or adamant, to find the world a spirit,
And wear my head, denying that I wear it.

" What a sublime discovery 'twas to make the
Universe universal egotism!
That all's ideal—all ourselves; I'll stake the
World (be it what you will) that *that's* no schism."

* Don Juan XI. 1, 2.

Idealism, while it cannot be beaten on its own ground, is nevertheless unable to account for the facts of reality. It cannot be refuted, yet it explains nothing. Materialism on the other hand is weakest at home. As a philosophy it is poor, but as a theory for practical explanations it is strong.

Materialism has been very successful when applied to natural phenomena, even to the explanation of psychological or other problems. But it could not be defended if attacked in its own province. Matter itself remained unexplained and, as a matter of consequence, materialists dropped into mysticism, declaring that matter itself was the ultimate mystery unsolved and unsolvable.

The weak point of materialism is that it identifies matter and reality. It starts with the assumption that all phenomena must be explained from the mechanical motion of inert matter. Man is a mere machine, an aggregate of molecules, the movements of which are produced through a *vis a tergo*, by push. Since, in the natural sciences, mechanical explanations prove of great value, Professor A. Lange proposed in his "History of Materialism" that science should continue to work out the solutions of problems as if materialism were correct, but at the same time we should know that from a critical and philosophical standpoint it is untenable ground.

The reason of this strange opposition between Idealism (or rather Spiritualism) and Materialism must be sought for in the consistency of one-sidedness which is found in both views. Neither spiritualism, *i. e.* idealism in its most advanced shape, nor materialism (the exaggeration of realism) can properly combine the parts of subjective and objective existence. Both views therefore are deficient in their explanation of the elementary data of psychical life. Spirit is declared to be a mere function of matter by materialists, but the impossibility that feeling can originate from dead and inert matter is passed over in silence. On the other side matter is declared to be a mere illusion of spirit, but the fact that matter is eternal in all changes while the ego of our consciousness possesses only a transient existence, is carefully ignored.

The unitary conception of the world alone can bridge over the chasm between the subjective and the objective. Monism acknowledges that the thinking subject is a part of its objective world, it is an object among other objects. Whatever differences obtain between them, they possess many features in common and one feature common to all nature is its spontaneity. While the origin of psychical life from absolutely dead matter is an impossibility, we can see no theoretical difficulty in considering the life of organisms as a special form of, and a particular phenomenon among, other spontaneous processes of nature.

The problem concerning the Origin of Psychical Life, has not yet been solved by biologists, but there is no reason why in time it should not be solvable.

It is not improbable that feeling will be demonstrated as a special kind of reflex-action in organized substance. The most common and best observable reflex-actions are visible motions which we can clearly perceive to be reactions against irritations. But if the visible motion is arrested somehow, if it is retained in the organism of living substance, the effect of the irritation can not have entirely disappeared in order to reappear upon some other occasion as if created out of nothing. The will of man has indeed often been credited with having this self-creative power that it can rise with all its wonderful energy out of empty non-existence. This is an illusion, for every act of willing is a reflex-action although it may have been stored up in the brain for years.

The visible motion of reflex-actions is no feeling. Feeling, it seems, can only be produced through an inhibition of the visible reflex motion. It appears as a kind of arrested and therefore inner motion. Certain kinds of feeling are perhaps justly called 'emotions' and 'commotions.' The origin of feeling may be comparable to the creation of heat and light. Heat and light also are inner, are molecular motions and can be produced by the arrest of visible motion.

This view receives a corroboration from the fact that feeling and visible motion are two distinct processes in animal beings. Wherever they appear together they must be considered as a combination rather than as a unity. The experiments of the modern psychologists of France prove that in such cases feeling is a superadded element. Under the spell of anæsthetics (for instance, of alcohol), or in a pathological condition, a man may act automatically in his wonted ways without being in possession of consciousness, and vice versa, a man suffering from aboulia may have the consciousness of his will but, although the muscles of his body are unimpaired, he is not able to execute his will;* he cannot let the intention of his consciousness pass into action. Consciousness and action, feeling and visible reflex motions, are distinct phenomena.

Idealism confines its world to the phenomena of feeling; materialism cannot explain their origin. According to Monism feeling is a process that, like other

* See Ribot, Diseases of the Will.

natural processes, takes place under certain conditions and disappears if these conditions disappear or arc counteracted.

Our feelings are only part of our existence. They are as it were the surface only, where many things appear that have their origin in the unknown depths. Many results come to light, of processes that never enter into the range of man's individual consciousness.

Man's consciousness is like a light that illumines the world of his existence, but does not create it. Our body, not otherwise than a plant, grows and forms itself without the interference of consciousness. So our social institutions grow, so our religions, and philosophies, and ideals develop independently of purposive interference and often contrary to directions consciously imparted.

Let us use the light of our consciousness as best we can. It serves the purpose of orientation. In the dark we can only grope, but where a light is lit we can survey our paths and need not go astray.

HEDONISM AND ASCETICISM.

A SYSTEMATIC conception of the universe is the theoretical, and ethics the practical aspect of philosophy. It is obvious that both are closely associated; the one is the basis of the other, and we cannot properly judge of the problems of the latter unless we have grasped the main truths of the former.

By "morals" we understand the proper conduct of life, and by "ethics" the science of morals. Now, it is true that a man can instinctively lead a moral life without having any knowledge of the theoretical basis and the practical application of ethics. Morals are, as a rule, very stable, and a moral man who in later years happens to believe in a wrong system of ethics is not liable to change much of his good habits of life. It is also true that a man who has inborn, perhaps hereditarily ingrained, immoral tendencies will by theoretical instruction in ethics most likely not be greatly improved. Nevertheless, as a rule, philosophy and ethics go together, and a wrong philosophy will produce a wrong ethics, and a wrong ethics will, if not in the present, certainly in the next generation, corrupt the morals also.

The details of a philosophy, or a religion (which latter, after all, is but a popular philosophy, a philosophy of the heart) may be, and, indeed, are, quite indifferent as to the ethical inferences that can be drawn from it. But the main truths are not. The main truths of a re-

ligion or philosophy lend the color to the ethics that
grows therefrom. And we find in the history of philosophy that materialism, with a great regularity, produces hedonism or utilitarianism; for it places the ultimate object of life in material existence and its well
being, *viz.* in happiness. Spiritualism, on the other
hand, as a rule, leads to asceticism; it renounces the
pleasures of the world, for it seeks the object of life in
the deliverance of the soul from the fetters of the body.
Monism rejects both views; it finds the purpose of
existence in the constant aspiration of realizing a higher
and better, a nobler, and more beautiful state of existence. Life is a boon so far only as it offers an occasion
to improve that which lies in our power to change—
the forms of things and the modes of life. It is not
pleasure or happiness that gives value to our days, but
the work done for the progress of our race. Moses expresses this truth most powerfully in a passage of his
grand psalm, which we quote according to the forci-
ble translation of Luther: "Man's life will last three
score years and ten, or, at the best, four score; but if
it was precious, it was of labor and sorrow."

Mere happiness will leave the heart empty, and the
aspiration for happiness will make of man a shallow
trifler. Asceticism, on the other hand, will prove destructive and suicidal. But if we consider the punct-
ual performance of our daily duty, every one in his
province, as the object of our lives, which must be
done to enhance our ideals and help mankind (be it
ever so little) to progress, we shall find occasion to
unite the truths hidden in both,—the materialistic and
spiritualistic ethics. We shall find sufficient occasion
to practice abstinence, to exercise self-control, and to
set aside the fleeting pleasures of the moment. At

the same time, while the pleasure-seeker will be wrecked in his vain endeavors, we shall experience that a noble satisfaction, which is the highest kind of happiness imaginable, follows those who are least concerned about enjoyment, and steadily attend to their duty.

`CAUSATION AND FREE WILL.

Two views have ever stood opposed to each other in the realm of religious and philosophical questions: the one claiming absolute determinism in the province of causation as a matter of course for all phenomena of nature and life, human actions not excluded; the other maintaining that whatever be the claim of determinism in the province of physical science, man's actions are *not* determined, for man is endowed with free will. The former opinion is generally considered as the scientific, the latter as the moral or religious view.

It is apparent that the very existence of morals and religion depends upon man's having a free will, and at the same time that determinism full and unrestricted, without any exceptions, is the condition of all science. The conciliation of both views is indeed the fundamental problem of all ethics. The idea of a free will in contradiction to the necessity of natural law is the last and perhaps the strongest redoubt of dualism. Two well-established truths here face one another, and appear irreconcilable,—for the *ought* in our breasts, our moral consciousness, we gladly confess, is an undeniable fact. And this *ought*, or, as the great sage of Königsberg calls it, " the categoric imperative " in us, postulates that man is a moral being, and that he has a free will. This free will, men of a dualistic bias think, is irreconcilable with the idea of the unison of all truths, which is the basic doctrine of monism.

Dualism (*i. e.*, spiritual dualism) which takes the view that two worlds exist independent of each other, —the spiritual world and the material world,—does not object to determinism in the material world, but it vigorously asserts that free will obtains in the spiritual world.

Materialism, in opposition to spiritual dualism, claims that freedom of will is a sham, that man has no free will, because his actions are determined throughout by law.

If spiritual dualism is right, scientific truth has very little value; for science exists only in so far as natural phenomena are, by strictest necessity, determined with regularity, and do not happen according to hazard or chance. If materialism is right in saying that man's freedom of will is a self-delusion, it would be ridiculous to speak of morals, and ethics (the science of morals) would be a self-contradiction.

Prof. James, of Harvard University,* accepts the dualistic view as best adapted to a moral teacher. He says: "We postulate indeterminism in the interests of the reality of our moral life, just as we postulate determinism in the interests of that of our scientific life."

Monism accepts determinism wholly and fully. But from the same standpoint of monism, free will must also be accepted as the basis of moral life. We deny that the issue is determinism *or* free will. In opposition to spiritual and material dualisms, we propound determinism *and* free will. We maintain that moral truth and scientific truth, that religion and science, regularity according to law and free will, are not irreconcilable contradictions. They are oppositions complementary to and explanatory of each other. If one is con-

* In a letter to THE OPEN COURT, published in No. 33, page 889.

ceived without taking the other into consideration, our view will be one-sided and insufficient. Both together form the monistic view, in which science and religion find their reconciliation.

Religious teachers usually adhere to the dogma of free will, while the philosophers of " matter and motion" do not accept this doctrine, but proclaim it to be in contradiction to the unyielding law of causality. The religious teachers know, that if there were no freedom of will, ethics would not exist; for it is freedom that implies responsibility for one's actions. On the other hand, Materialism as a rule annihilates ethics at its root and establishes in its stead such rules of conduct as will ensure the greatest amount of happiness.

Now, according to the law of causality, the actions of man result through the same necessity as any event or phenomenon. It is a strange confusion to make of necessity and freedom a contradictory opposition, so that either would exclude the other. If a man can do as he pleases, we call him free; but if he is prohibited from following motives which stir him, if by some *restraint* or *compulsion* he is limited, he is not free. But every man, whether under certain conditions he be free or restrained, under exactly these and no other circumstances must will, of necessity, just as he does will, and not otherwise. As to this there is no doubt, if causality is truly the universal law of the world.

The actions of free will are just as much regulated by law as any other natural phenomena. The moral *ought* certainly involves a *can*. Two men under the very same conditions *can* act differently; but a man of a certain character and under certain conditions, if he is free, will necessarily act in accordance with his character and not otherwise.

Those who maintain that free will and determinism are irreconcilable contradictions start from the apparently slight but important error that *compulsion* and *necessity* are identical. They think that what happens from necessity proceeds from compulsion somehow. They overlook the fact that there is a necessity imposed from without as well as a necessity operating from within: the former acts by compulsion, from outward mechanical pressure as it were; while the latter works spontaneously, though necessarily, in accordance with the character of the man, constituting his free will. For instance, a man delivers to a highwayman his valuables because he is compelled to do so by threats or even blows; he suffers violence; his action is not free. But if a man, seeing one of his wretched fellow-beings suffering from hunger and cold through extreme poverty, and overpowered by compassion gives away all he has about him, this man does not act under compulsion. He acts from free will, but being such as he is, he so acts of necessity, in accordance with his character.

Where compulsion exists, free will is annihilated; but necessity need not be compulsion. Whoever is unable to make this distinction between compulsion and necessity, will never get a clear insight into the theory of free will. Necessity is the inevitable sequence by which a certain result follows according to a certain law. It is the internal harmony and logical order of the world. Compulsion, however, is an external restraint, and a foreign pressure exercised to check and hinder by violence. Give the magnet freedom on a pivot, and it will, of necessity, turn toward the north, according to the qualities or properties of magnetism. But if you direct it by a pressure of the finger to some other point, you will exercise some compulsion, which does not allow it to show its real nature and quality. Were the magnet endowed with sentiment and gifted with the power of speech, it would say in the first case: " I am free, and of my free will I point toward the north." In the second case, however, it would feel that it was acted upon and forced into some other direction against its nature, and would declare its freedom to be curtailed.

It is the same with man; and the moral worth of a man depends entirely upon what motives direct his will. An ethical estimate of moral actions is not possible, except under the condition that they are the expression and realization of free will. Freedom is the *sine qua non* of morality and moral responsibility. But the best action would amount to nothing if it were a mere chance result which, like a throw at dice, might have occured otherwise. And if the free actions of man were not regulated by law, if free will meant that a man of certain character under certain conditions could act otherwise than he does, if free will were identical with chance, if, in a word, free will were indeterminism, this kind of free will would not only destroy science but morals and ethics also. The whole value of any moral deed rests on the fact that the man *could not*, under the conditions, act otherwise than thus, that it was an act of *free will*, and, at the same time, of inevitable *necessity*.

The interests of " moral life " and of " scientific life " thus appear from the standpoint of monism as two aspects of one truth, in which both find their explanation. The dualistic solution of the problem will prove destructive of both views; for dualistic science and dualistic ethics must in mutual annihilation play the parts of the famous Kilkenny cats. Monism teaches that the moral view and the scientific view are two different aspects, although their object may be one and the same thing. A psychologist, a physician, or a lawyer may view the actions of a man from a scientific standpoint; and a clergyman, a preacher of morals, or a historian, or a biographer, or the critic of an author, may contemplate the very same actions from a moral standpoint. Should we then, in the former case, take to determinism, and in the latter to indeterminism,—or shall we, by excluding human actions from the province of determinism, entirely annihilate ethics as a science?

Indeterminism is unthinkable in science as well as in morals; it would make every action a morally indifferent and scientifically indeterminable phenomenon.

Free will and determinism do not exclude each other. Free will is the postulate of morals, determinism is the postulate of science. The actions of a free will are not irregular or without law; they are rigidly determined by the character of the man that acts.

———————

FORMAL THOUGHT AND ETHICS

The most remarkable treatise on ethics as a science is Immanuel Kant's "Foundation of the Metaphysics of Morality." (*Grundlegung zur Metaphysik der Sitten.*) He attempts in this little book to show that the rules of moral conduct can be based on an unalterable principle, which by rational beings can and must be recognized as being of universal application. Kant says:

"As pure mathematics is distinguished from applied mathematics and pure logic from applied logic, so may the pure philosophy (the metaphysics) of ethics be distinguished from the applied philosophy of ethics, that is, as applied to human nature. By this distinction of terms it at once appears that ethical principles are not based upon the peculiarities of human nature, but that they must be existent by themselves a priori,—whence, for human nature, as well as for any rational nature, practical rules can be derived."

We prefer to call Kant's Metaphysics of Morality* "Formal Ethics." Formal ethics is as truly the basis of applied ethics as for instance geometry is the basis of geodesy. Formal ethics is a science as demonstrable and plain as logic or arithmetic, and like the other formal sciences will find its verification and application in experience.

---

* We here briefly review Kant's ethics in so far only as we agree, and abstain from a discussion in so far as we do not agree. Some of Kant's ideas, and more so his terminology admit of criticism. For instance, his conception of freedom is vague, and his discrimination between man as *homo noumenon* or a moral being, and man as *homo phænomenon* or a physical being, can not be conceded in the sense he puts it.

Kant says :

"Will is conceived as a power of determining itself to action in accordance with the conception of certain laws. And such a power can only be met with in rational beings. Now it is the end that serves the will as the objective ground of its self-determination, and *this end, if fixed by reason alone*, must hold equally good for all rational creatures. * * *

"To know what I have to do in order that my volition be good, requires on my part no far-reaching sagacity. Unexperienced in respect of the course of nature, unable to be prepared for all the occurrences transpiring therein, I simply ask myself : Canst thou will, that the maxim of thy conduct may become a universal law ? Where it can not become a universal law, there the maxim of thy conduct is reprehensible, and that, too, not by reason of any disadvantage consequent thereupon to thee or even others, but because it is not fit to enter as a principle into a possible enactment of universal laws."

Kant formulates his maxim in the following way :

"Act so as if the maxim of thy conduct by thy volition were to become a natural law."

If a maxim of conduct is fit to enter as a principle into a possible enactment of universal laws, it will be found in harmony with cosmical laws ; if not, it must come in conflict with the order of things in the universe. It then cannot stand, and will, if persistently adhered to, lead (perhaps slowly but inevitably) to a certain ruin.

A will that as a matter of principle determines itself to be guided by reason alone, and thus to remain in unison with the order of the universe, Kant calls a *good will*. The command prescribed by pure reason is the "*categoric imperative.*" He calls it "categoric" because its behests admit of no exception, and are to be applied with rigid universality. Since there is only one kind of reason, there is only one measure or standard of morality, which must be the same for all rational beings. A *"person,"* according to Kant, is an individual who can be held responsible for his acts. A person can by the power of his reason regulate his action according to principles, and the subject-matter to which in special cases the categoric imperative obliges or binds us, is called *"duty."*

The enormous practical importance of formal thought appears here in its full significance. All formal truths are necessary truths ; they possess universality, and therefore they can be employed as norms. In other words, they are ethological; they can be used as rules and constitute a categorical *ought.* Ethics is, as it were, the logic of man's conduct, and vice versa; logic may be considered as the ethics of thinking. Geometry is the ethics of measuring and arithmetic the ethics of calculation. Without formal thought and without the rigidity of the laws of formal thought, we could have no constitutive norms whatever, no basis for scientific investigation, no guidance for invention, and no foundation of ethics.

*   *   *

Before Kant arrived at his ethics, he had tried to explain morality from man's desire for happiness.* But he abandoned this idea entirely; and certainly, morals can not be identified with our desire for happiness, although it is true that immorality always causes much misfortune, and will, as a rule, lead to unhappiness. In fact, morals are preached in order to counteract the dangers of our desire for happiness. The highroad of virtue does not appear at all pleasurable, nor does it promise ever to become so, while the by-paths of vice are extremely pleasant to look upon, and many

* *Werke* viii, p. 676, and iii, p. 392.

of them will continue to be so for a long time, perhaps even to the end ; and the end may be a sudden and painless death.

Happiness is like a shadow; if pursued it will flee from us; but if a man does not trouble himself about it, and strictly attends to his duties, pleasures of the best and noblest kind will crop out everywhere in his path. If he does not anxiously pursue it, happiness will follow him.

Happiness in itself, the quickened pulse of joy, the gladness of heart, and the laughter of our lips is a shallow and empty thing; it has no value, and the man who attended to his duty for the mere pleasure of having the consciousness that he has done his duty, would find his reward poor. He must attend to his duty for the sake of his duty, and he will realize that it is not happiness itself that blesses us, but the object which causes our happiness ; it is not the joyous thrill as such, but the ideas, the hopes, the aspirations that joyfully thrill through the fibres of our mental existence. Accordingly, we should not so much care for happiness and for a great amount of happiness, but that our desire for happiness be satisfied with, and respond to, such motives only as possess moral value —such as are in harmony with the universal order of things.

*   *   *

Although we accept Kant's formal ethics as the basis of morality, thus attributing the highest authority in matters of conduct to reason, we do not in the least undervalue the importance of experience as a source of information concerning our moral aspirations. And although we maintain that, as there is but one reason, so there is but one standard of morality, we do not deny that there are many different stages and innumerable aberrations in the moral development of mankind. The abstract conception of a good will is always one and the same, being the unison of will with reason, but the conception of that which is to be looked upon as good, must necessarily vary not only with the kind and amount of reason we possess, but also with the changeable demands of the circumstances in which we live. Different conditions require different duties; and to different duties different moral ideals correspond.

Usually we are inclined to judge the actions of men of past times from the standpoint of the moral ideals of to-day. But that is entirely wrong, and many apparently barbarous deeds are justifiable—even right, with regard to the circumstances and requirements of their era. If some hero of olden times had acted according to the higher and better ideal of these latter days, it would have been considered (and sometimes perhaps justly so) as weakness on his part. For though the ethical tendency is the same throughout, yet the evolution of ethical ideals shows different stages.

*   *   *

The innate qualities and talents with which nature endows certain individuals, and which therefore are justly called gifts, according to the theory of evolution, are faculties inherited from ancestors. The labor of former generations is not lost; its fruit has been preserved and handed down to the generation now living.

This fact has a profound ethical import!

There is nothing without work in this world. That easy and apparently effortless production which we admire in genius, is possible only through the inherited abilities acquired by the labor of ancestors.

The single individual, therefore, ought to be conscious of being the product of the labor of ages. And what he does, be it evil or good, will live after him in so far as his individuality impresses itself and influences his contemporaries. In consideration of this fact, man will think with reverence of the past, with regard for the future, and with earnestness of the present.

*   *   *

The categorical imperative of Kant appears as a norm or a regulative law which is of universal validity just as much as the norms of arithmetic or logic. All the rules of formal sciences have a normative, *i. e.*, a regulative value.

If they are rigidly applied, they will in all cases be found to be correct and to lead us to true results. The categoric imperative, however, (not unlike the norms of the other formal sciences,) is more than a mere regulative law; it is a natural law which rules the development of the world and is the cause of all progress in the history of evolution. We can verify its presence through an impartial observation of facts by experience.

Human society could not even exist, nor could it ever have risen into existence, if the moral 'ought' did not constantly prompt the majority of human minds to obey the behests of the categoric imperative. No society is possible unless it is founded upon the basis of morality.

Morality, although in a broader sense of the word, extends far beyond the province of rational beings. It does not only regulate the relations among them, it also creates the conditions from which they originate.

Cells possess all properties of organized beings:

alimentation, growth, and propagation. A mother-cell, having reproduced itself by repeated divisions, is still connected with its filial cells. All cells in their union are more fit to encounter the struggle for existence. Henceforth the work to be done for their preservation is divided and dispensed in such a way that some cells perform one, other cells an other function for the unity thus created. It is division of work, according to a general plan; and that is what constitutes an organism.

The single organ or limb of a body does no longer exist for itself but serves the idea of a larger unity of which it feels itself to be a part. The purpose, aim, and end of its existence is forthwith not in itself but in something higher than itself. This principle pervades all organized nature. Organisms cannot exist but under this condition. The relations of the different organs of an organism among themselves demand special kinds of work to be done, which, if the organs were conscious, we would not hesitate to call their duties. The organs of an organism, if in a state of health, obey this principle, and this principle is essentially a moral principle.

The same principle which produced organisms and animals, guides them in their further development; and only so far as any creature is animated by this ethical guidance, is it able to develop into some higher being. The moral principle is the star of Bethlehem that guides the foremost men of all human races to the cradle where a new truth and new duties are born and where the germs of new ideas are thriving.

The human body and the organism of society both rest on the same principle. The first higher unity is the family; families grow into tribes, and tribes form nations. The love of parents has broadened into patriotism, and no doubt the next higher ideal will be that of humanity.

The next higher stage to which natural development ever tends is its ideal, and there will be no rest in the minds of the single individuals until this ideal is realized. After that, new ideals arise and lead us onward on the interminable, infinite path of progress, not as Darwin says, merely driven by the famous law of the struggle for life, but prompted by the strife for the ideal.

The ethical principle is no mere constitutional law, proposed by a legislature as fitted to serve the majority. It is, as we have learned, a natural law pervading the universe ; and a scientist must be blind to facts if he does not discover it. Even in the inorganic world, I venture to say, this law prevails, though in a broader sense. Gravitation out of a whirlpool of gaseous materials forms well-arranged solar systems. It is the law of order and unity which dispenses to different bodies the different parts to be performed. The law of gravity, as formulated in mathematical terms by Newton, is the ethical rule of primordial matter ; and if the single atoms of a nebula which are still rushing in different directions, could tell us their ideal, it would be that of a harmoniously regulated solar system. The chaos will clear, according to simple mechanical rules ; the ideal will be realized, and the general turmoil will give way to order.

* * *

This world is not a world of happiness, but of ethical aspiration. The essence of all existence is evolution or a constant realization of new ideals. True, it is the struggle for life; but if you look at it more closely, is it really life that the progressive part of humanity is striving for? No, they sacrifice even their lives for some higher purpose, for their ideal. If we look upon the martyrs of progress, it would indeed be a strange contradiction to say that people are consciously sacrificing and losing their lives in a struggle for life.

The ideal is erroneously supposed to be an imaginary nonenity; or the illusion of an enthusiastic—perhaps even a morbid brain. An ideal, however, is a part of our soul, and it is such as prompts us to action, and can regulate all our conduct in life. The power and importance of ideals is greatly increased because it can easily be imparted to others in a few words. A martyr may die, but his heroism can at the same time be impressed on the minds of his very hangmen, so that the best part of his soul is implanted into their souls, and triumphs through the sacrifice of his life.

Ideals are the most intense realities imaginable. Physically considered, they are certain organized structures in a living brain. The mechanical work done by the combustion of the oxygen in a few drops of blood is extremely small, and how great, incalculably great, is the result obtained! Here is the δός μοι ποῦ στῶ καὶ κινήσω τὴν γῆν* of which Archimedes spoke. The thinking of an ideal may not cost more expenditure of energy than 0.001 foot-pound, and yet it may revolutionize the world.

The ideal is no mere fiction, it is a power of reality, pervading the universe as a law of nature; and

* Translated : Give me a place to stand on and I will move the world.

with regard to humanity it points out to man the path
of progress.   Progress, if it is guided by the ideal,
will produce new and better eras for humankind. And
if a moral tendency were not the fundamental law of
nature, there could not be any advancement, development, or evolution.

THE ONENESS OF MAN AND NATURE.*

ACCORDING to Monism man is a part of Nature, a part of the one great All, and the ethical import of Monism is based on the recognition of this idea of oneness. The barrier which in the opinion of dualistic systems existed between the ego and the rest of the world is broken down. The individual belongs to the whole as an integral part of it. The more fully, the more correctly and truly the cosmos† of the Universe is mirrored in a consciousness, the closer will be the union of the ego with the All, and the more moral the individual must become. The better a man understands the true connection of his soul with the souls of his fellow-beings, and the better he comprehends his right relation to the great whole of all-existence, the more will he conform to what he calls the laws of sociology and the moral rules of conduct. And the more he conforms to these conditions, the fitter he will be to survive in the struggle for existence.

This is, in outline, the ethical aspect of Monism, and this is the character of evolution also. The ethics of Monism can fitly be named Evolutionism, for evolution is possible only because the laws of the world in which we live, are a moral power. The Cosmos itself, the order of the world, is the foundation of morality. Properly speaking, we cannot say that the Cosmos, or the All, or God, is moral. This is an

* Written in answer to an essay of Mr. Moncure D. Conway.
† *Cosmos* literally translated means *order*.

anthropomorphic expression, which, in poetic speech, may be allowable, but is not correct. The truth is individuals are moral in so far as they conform with the Cosmos, in so far as they become one with the All and conform to its order, or humanly speaking, as they obey the laws of the whole.

Mr. Conway says:

" Where is any moral law found in nature except in man ? Except in man, and in so much of the world as man has partly humanized, nature seems predatory, and cruelly impartial between good and evil, brier and the fruit—if not, indeed, favorable to the brier. May it not be more truly said that there is a moral law in man to which nature must conform in order to live well and be blessed ? "

From the monistic standpoint man is the highest product of the All. Man is the blossom on the tree of nature, and humanity is its fruit. .Man is grander and nobler than the rest of nature, as the blossom is a higher stage of evolution than the leaf. But a flower and a leaf, though they may be contrasted as the higher and lower stages of one and the same plant, cannot be considered as two essentially different beings. Thus human civilization, and the vegetable and animal kingdoms, can be viewed under the aspect of opposites, but not as contradictories. Both are products of the same tree, both are natural, and we shall find that in human society the same fundamental laws are at work as in the other natural kingdoms. Man by his higher qualifications conforms more quickly and readily to these laws. There is more truth in his conception of the universe than in the imperfect percepts of animal brains. Therefore he is more powerful, therefore he is more moral, and therefore fitter to survive in the struggle for existence.

These facts cannot be denied when we observe how man takes possession of the earth and how brutes and wild beasts are extirpated; how also among men the savage races die out, while the civilized nations conquer the world. And yet it is an every day's experience that the morally bad triumph over the good, and that the honest are worsted by the wicked. The possibility of falling into error is greater than that of hitting the truth: accordingly while one truth is born, hundreds of errors have occasion to arise. Errors multiply quicker than truth and the briers seem more fertile than the useful fruit-trees.

The truth of this is obvious, although the potency of wickedness seems to contradict flatly the former statement that morality makes man fitter to survive. Similarly, the fertility of error seems irreconcilable with the fact that truth is stronger than error and must survive in a world where the fittest will finally conquer. And if we experience, ourselves, the power of iniquity, if we personally suffer from the advantages which the wicked gain by their very unscrupulousness, we are but too much inclined to lose all confidence in the moral order of the world.

There have been and still are times of trial and tribulation in the development of entire nations as well as of single individuals, when it takes all our strength not to lose faith in ethics and in the worth of ethics. Even Christ cried out, in the agony of death, his *Eli, Eli, lama sabachthani.* "My God, my God, why hast thou forsaken me?" All the sages of humanity agree that it takes a strong character and the moral power of purpose, faithfully to endure in temptation and constantly to trust in truth and righteousness. There is sufficient cause for a lack of faith, and enough

occasion for following the path of vice and wrong-
doing. Almost all aberrations from truth and justice
appear pleasant and full of promise at the start, and
the warnings of parents and teachers are easily forgotten. Nevertheless these aberrations lead to inevit
able ruin, and although the righteous path may be
thorny now and then, perhaps too often for our taste,
we should nevertheless, difficult though it may be,
never lose faith in the final triumph of truth and
justice.

The spirited shepherd boy who became king of
Judea sings in one of the psalms:

> The wicked in his pride doth prosecute the poor.
>
> His mouth is full of cursing and deceit and fraud; under his
> tongue is mischief and vanity.
>
> He sitteth in the lurking places of the villages: in the secret
> doth he murder the innocent: his eyes are privily set against the
> poor.
>
> He lieth in wait secretly as a lion in his den: he lieth in wait
> to catch the poor: he doth catch the poor, when he draweth him
> into his net.
>
> He croucheth, and humbleth himself, that the poor may fall
> by his strong ones.
>
> He hath said in his heart, God hath forgotten: he hideth his
> face; he will never see it.

And in another song the royal Hebrew poet gives
an answer to his anxious doubts as to the apparent
lack of justice in the order of the world. He says:

> Fret not thyself because of evildoers, neither be thou envious
> against the workers of iniquity.
>
> For they will soon be cut down like the grass, and wither as
> the green herb.
>
> Cease from anger, and forsake wrath; fret not thyself in any
> wise to do evil.
>
> For yet a little while, and the wicked shall not be: yea, thou
> shalt diligently consider his place, and it shall not be.

But the meek shall inherit the earth; and shall delight themselves in the abundance of peace.

The wicked plotteth against the just and gnasheth upon him with his teeth.

The wicked have drawn out the sword, and have bent their bow, to cast down the poor and needy, and to slay such as be of upright conversation.

Their sword shall enter into their own heart, and their bows shall be broken,

A little that a righteous man hath is better than the riches of many wicked.

The wicked borroweth, and payeth not again: but the rightous showeth mercy, and giveth.

I have seen the wicked in great power, and spreading himself like a green bay tree.

Yet he passed away, and, lo, he was not: yea, I sought him but he could not be found.

I have been young, and now am old; yet have I not seen the righteous forsaken, nor his seed begging bread.

Depart from evil, and do good; and dwell for evermore.

The righteous shall inherit the land, and dwell therein for ever.

David finds comfort in observing the eventual fate of the prosperous evil-doer,—for " a little while " and " he passed away and, lo, he was not."

The triumph of truth and virtue, however, is not such as to make their devotees wander through the pleasant vales of perpetual happiness. Just the contrary; the path of virtue and truth is often not easy to find and difficult to walk upon. " Strait is the gate and narrow is the way which leadeth unto life and few there be that find it." Similarly the Greek poet says:

Τῆς δ'ἀρετῆς ἱδρῶτα θεοὶ προπάροιθεν ἔθηκαν
Ἀθάνατοι · μακρὸς δὲ καὶ ὄρθιος οἶμος ἐπ' αὐτήν.

[Toil before Virtue is placed by judicious decrees of Immortals. Steep is the path to her heights and rugged the road to the summit.]

The evil consequences of error, folly, and crime, it is true, often come so slowly that it appears as if the sinner would escape punishment. They come late, yet they are sure to come, as a Greek sage has said:

ὀψέ θεῶν ἀλέουσι μύλοι, ἀλέουσι δὲ λεπτά.*

"Though the mills of God grind slowly,
Yet they grind exceeding small;
Though with patience he stands waiting,
With exactness grinds he all."†

The simple narrative of the crucifixion of Christ has impressed humanity so deeply because of the moral lesson is conveys. The most touching and sympathetic features of the holy legend must be found in the suffering which the God in man has to undergo. The divinity of man is a source of intense pain and tribulation. Our very ideals lead us into trouble and temptation and even into the darkness of death. And yet we should not despair; we should preserve our faith in truth and righteousness. It is this lesson which made of the tragedy of Golgotha, a gospel and glad tidings to the struggling and despairing human race.

It is true, that with the new revelation of Christianity *per crucem ad lucem*, which showed that the path of righteousness leads through suffering, and that only a crown of thorns can become a crown of glory—errors arose which retarded or seemed to retard the general progress of truth. The same had happened to Buddhism. Its true ethical idea was soon overgrown and smothered by errors. Buddha himself, and in a similar manner Christ himself, opposed the dualistic and pessimistic conceptions of their forerunners,

---

* Sextus Empiricus.

† The English version by Longfellow is a translation of Friedrich von Logau's epigram:

Gottes Mühlen mahlen langsam,
Mahlen aber trefflich klein;
Ob aus Langmuth er sich säumet,
Bringt mit Schärf' er Alles ein.

the one of the Sankya philosophy, the other of the Essenes. Both for a time observed the prescripts of the sects from which they arose. Then both opposed the Asceticism practiced by their predecessors without falling into the error of hedonism. Both rejected fasting as injurious to body and soul, both left the abodes in deserts and abandoned monkish habits. They lived as men among men, they sat down at table and ate and drank with the sinners. The disciples of St. John therefore began to grow doubtful as to the divine mission of Jesus. They sent word to him and asked: "Art thou he that should come or do we look for another."

Christ, as well as Buddha, represents a reaction against pessimism. It was the start of a new faith, a new hope, a new religion, a religion that should bear the features of meliorism. These melioristic features in Christian ethics, which beam forth in Faith and Hope and Charity, have been the strength of Christianity and did most for its propagation. It is the Christian faith that conquered the world, not the pessimistic and world-despising despair of its dualism.

The tares grow with the wheat, and errors freely sprout where a new truth is conceived. Errors multiply and increase more luxuriantly than truth does. And yet it is only for a while; they will pass away and truth will stand forth victorious.

It was again the Christian faith, the melioristic feature of Christianity, that proved a regenerative power in the time of the Reformation and led humanity one step nearer to a monistic, a unitary, and a harmonious conception of the All. It is faith in ethics and confidence in our ideals that, by an abandonment of creed, will lead humanity to the purer heights of a nobler conception of life and a more elevated existence on earth.

The ethical aspect of Monism has been brought to light more strongly by the recent investigations of experimental psychology, which have been instituted in France by M. Th. Ribot and other investigators. The modern psychology of M. Ribot agrees well with the monistic view that has been propounded by German scientists. The dualistic conception, that there is at the bottom of the soul such a thing as an ego, has been proved to be wrong. The ego, or the state of consciousness, is not an entity which produces our mental life; on the contrary, it is the result of the innumerable and complicated nerve-organisms in our body. The thoughts we think are the elements of which our mental life consists. Our mind is *de facto* a republic of ideas, of which now the one and now the other is called into activity. The unity of mental activity is no proof of Descartes's view that the soul is a simple being ; for the unity of the mind is now considered as resulting from a rich and complicated system.

The ego of our consciousness is concentrated and centralized, according to M. Ribot, in a similar way as our sight is focused in the lenses of our eyes. Prof. Mach compares the personality of an individual to an indifferent symbolical thread on which are strung the valuable pearls of our real existence.* These pearls are the ideas which that entered into our brains. The ideas that live in us are our true Self. These ideas we have received from others and we communicate to others. These ideas, in so far as they are ideals, warm

* Prof. Ernst Mach, ''Transformation and Adaptation in Scientific Thought.'' THE OPEN COURT, Nos. 46 and 48.

our hearts and keep aglow our enthusiasm so as to make life worth living; for. life is only worth living if we aspire towards something that is greater and nobler than our limited ego. These ideas in so far as they are the essence of what we call humanity, make of every single man a representative of mankind.

Thus the barrier between the ego and the great whole of the All is broken. Prof. Mach* says : " Humanity in its entirety is like a polyp-plant. . The material and organic bonds of individual union have, indeed, been severed ; they would only have impeded freedom of movement and evolution. But the ultimate aim, the psychical connection of the whole, has been attained in a much higher degree through the more luxuriant development which has thus been made possible."

The individual man is ethical by his Oneness with humanity, and humanity is ethical by its Oneness with Nature. If humanity would cut itself loose from Nature in which its origin lies and which affords the condition of its existence, it would die away and wither like a tree that is severed from its root. Humanity as a whole, as well as the single man, can live and grow, advance and prosper, only by remaining one with the All, by being moral; *i. e.,* by observing and conforming to the cosmical order of Nature.

ETHICS AND NATURAL SCIENCE.

THE beginning of ethics is *thought*. The animal who cannot think or reason cannot be called an ethical being. When man begins to think, he commences to understand his relations to others and thus' learns his duties. He formulates his duties in general principles and regulates his actions according to maxims of universal application. In this way only can he place himself and his life in harmony with the order of All-existence.

When we reflect a moment upon what we owe our ancestors, we shall soon find that we owe them all we have and even more: we owe them all we *are*. What are we but the accumulated activity of all our ancestors from the very beginnings of life, the moner and the moner's struggles for existence included? Our nineteenth century civilization is not a revolution which has introduced any new idea that inverts or destroys the thoughts, ideas, or aspirations of former centuries. The most advanced view, however different from the old views, is a further evolution of the past.

The recognition of this truth is the essence of historical research, and those who are most advanced in the culture of true progress, who acknowledge the principle of scientific investigation in ethics and religion, those who are decided to modernize their morals and adapt themselves to the spirit of the dawning future, should be the first to understand this truth. Yet many radical thinkers overlook it. Through their opposition to the errors of the past they become blind to its merits. Only by understanding the connection of the present with the past will they be able to do justice to the cause which they defend, for they can gain justice for themselves only by doing justice to others, and the just claims of the present can only be established by showing that they are the logical outcome of the past.

Ethics is not, as some modern philosophers try to make us believe, an arithmetical example by which to calculate how we can purchase, at least sacrifice, the greatest amount of happiness. This barter morality of hedonism is a pseudo-ethics which indeed would make true ethics impossible.

The pseudo-ethics of hedonism starts from the wrong idea that man lives solely for being or becoming happy. If this were true, the great pessimist Schopenhauer would be right in saying that life is a failure and that existence is not desirable because a life without trouble and pain, a victory without battle, a conquest without wounds and anxiety, are impossible. Ethics is so much at variance with man's craving for happiness that if man lived merely to be happy there would be no ethics whatever. Ethics indeed is taught to counteract the dangerous, although perhaps inborn and natural, craving for happiness.

The beginning of ethics is to reflect upon ourselves, our surroundings, and our actions. Before we act we must stop to think. The brute animal follows his impulses; so does the savage. The thoughtful man takes into consideration all possible results of his action; and however dimly at first, he soon learns that his person is intimately connected with his surroundings, with his fellow-beings, and with nature.

Even a savage knows that he is no absolute entity, no unit by himself. His very existence is the product of his parents, and his life is sustained through certain natural conditions by a constant struggle in which he is aided or hindered by his fellow-men. His relation to his fellow-men, and his dependence upon nature which yields to him substance that maintains his life, teaches man that he has some duties to perform, which if neglected will prove disastrous to himself and his fellow-beings. The *relations* in which man stands to others imply *duties ;* and the man who attends to these duties is moral.

When man earnestly attends to what he recognizes as his duties, he will progress and in consequence thereof his comfort and prosperity will increase. His pleasures will be more refined ; his happiness, his enjoyments, and recreations will be better and nobler.

The increase, or rather refinement of happiness, however, cannot be considered as the ultimate aim of ethics, for pain and affliction increase at the same rate, because man's irritability, his susceptibility to pain, grows with the growth of his intellectuality.

The pain of a more civilized man will be more intense than that of a savage, -and it is an undeniable fact that people of a lower degree of culture are as a rule merrier than the more educated classes. There is sufficient occasion in this country to observe the glad and hearty happiness of the negro, who is so easily satisfied. In comparison with the African the more cultured American of European ancestry must appear morose.

If all the advancement of our civilization had no other object than to produce a greater amount of happiness, the anthropoids would have better remained in their forests and have lived upon the tropical trees, subsisting on their fruit. They would thereby have better attained this end. Therefore we maintain that the elevation of all human emotions, whether they are painful or happy, the elevation of man's whole existence, of his actions and aspirations, is the constant aim of ethics.

* * *

THE hostility which prevails between scientists on the one side and moral teachers on the other is produced through a misunderstanding. The moral teacher, and especially the clergyman, is afraid lest science undermine the principles of ethics. The doctrine of the survival of the fittest appears to contradict the principle of morality. And the scientist in his turn does not find the moral law as it is commonly preached in the pulpit, justified in nature.

Professor Huxley says:

"From the point of view of the moralist the animal world is on about the same level as a gladiator's show. The creatures are fairly well treated, and set to fight—whereby the strongest, the swiftest, and the cunningest live to fight another day. * * *

"In the cycle of phenomena presented by the life of man, no more moral end is discernible than in that presented by the lives of the wolf and of the deer. * * *

'As among these, so among primitive men, the weakest and stupidest went to the wall, while the toughest and shrewdest, those who were best fitted to cope with their circumstances, but not the best in any other sense, survived. * * *

Professor Huxley undervalues the use of morality in the struggle for existence. Man survived not because of his toughness, or his shrewdness, but because

of his moral qualities. The antediluvial fox was perhaps shrewder, and the lion or bear tougher, than the
prehistoric savage or man-ape ; but they were lacking
in the moral faculties which bind single individuals
together with the ties of love, of family, and of friend-
ship. Moral feelings, or rather the capacity and conditions of the growth of moral feelings, the tendency
to reveal moral qualities, made the primitive man
sociable. A social animal develops more morality than
solitary beings, and the shrewdness of a social being
becomes intelligence

Intelligence is more powerful as a weapon in the
struggle for existence than shrewdness, because it does
not lack in morality; it is more in unison with the
cosmic order. Human speech is the product of intelligence and not of shrewdness. Man was able to develop speech only because he was moral enough to be
social, and this morality elevated man above the rest
of the animal world. Among savage tribes the most
intelligent and *not* the shrewdest survived.

It is an undeniable fact that in any given district
the tribes who were lacking in morality, even when
the very shrewdest and toughest, had to go to the
wall, while in the end the more moral remained victorious.

It is a wrong historical view to imagine that the
Romans conquered the world because they were
shrewder, stronger, and more ferocious than their
neighbors. They conquered the world because they
possessed in addition to strength a rare moral quality
—the quality of justice. With regard to their exercise
of justice, indeed, they were by no means perfect ; but
they were more advanced, more moral, and better in
this respect than any other nation of their time, cul-

tured Greece not excepted. Yet even the strength of the Romans was not the physical force of a ferocious bull; it was the moral strength of courage.

It will thus be seen that morality affords the power to survive, and if the primitive savage was not moral in the present acceptation of the word, he was in his time relatively the most moral being on earth, and this gave him more strength than toughness or shrewdness could ever afford.

Prof. Huxley declares in other passages of the same essay:

"The history of civilization—that is, of society—on the other hand, is the record of the attempts which the human race has made to escape from this position. * * *

"But the effort of ethical man to work toward a moral end by no means abolished, perhaps has hardly modified, the deep-seated impulses which impel the natural man to follow his non-moral course." * * *

Professor Huxley adds with special reference to the civilization of the English nation of to-day:

"We not only are, but, under penalty of starvation, we are bound to be, a nation of shopkeepers. But other nations also lie under the same necessity of keeping shop, and some of them deal in the same goods as ourselves. Our customers naturally seek to get the most and the best in exchange for their produce. If our goods are inferior to those of our competitors, there is no ground compatible with the sanity of the buyers, which can be alleged, why they should not prefer the latter. And, if that result should ever take place on a large and general scale, five or six millions of us would soon have nothing to eat. We know what the cotton famine was; and we can therefore form some notion of what a dearth of customers would be.

"Judged by an ethical standard, nothing can be less satisfactory than the position in which we find ourselves. In a real, though incomplete, degree we have attained the condition of peace which is the main object of social organization (and it may, for argument's sake, be assumed that we desire nothing but that which

is in itself innocent and praiseworthy—namely, the enjoyment of
the fruits of honest industry). And lo ! in spite of ourselves, we
are in reality engaged in an internecine struggle for existence with
our presumably no less peaceful and well-meaning neighbors. We
seek peace and we do not ensue it. The moral nature in us asks
for no more than is compatible with the general good ; the non-
moral nature proclaims and acts upon that fine old Scottish family
motto, 'Thou shalt starve ere I want.' Let us be under no illusion, then."

If the unitary conception of the world is true, that
all existence is but one great continuous whole ; that
all difference is but variety in unity; that one truth
is in harmony with all other truths as every part of existence is related to the whole existence of the One and
All :—if this is true, how can there be a difference between the moralist's and the naturalist's views? Should
we not declare *a priori* that there can be no contradictory truths?   Either the naturalist or the moralist,
perhaps both, are wrong.

With all due respect to the facts presented by
Professor Huxley, we must object to the conclusion at
which he arrives. Professor Huxley's view of morals
is based on the error that the wolf is immoral while
the sheep is moral. The strong one is supposed to be
an evil-doer, simply on account of his strength, while the
weak one is supposed to be *good* simply on account of
his weakness. Not the hero is glorified that "fights
the good fight of faith," but the martyr that allows
himself to be slaughtered without resistance.

This ethics has long been fostered by Christian
moralists, because unfortunately Christ was compared
to a lamb that is sacrificed, and because, in one of his
allegories, Christ compares the good to sheep whom
he will place at the right hand. The allegory is mis-
interpreted. It is not the weakness, not the inactivity,

but the purity of the sheep that is approved by Christ. How much is blamed, in another parable, the inactive and cowardly servant who buried the talent that was entrusted to him!

This ovine morality has detracted much of the pith and strength from Christian ethics. It has made it tame and weak and even despicable. Morality is not as many lamb-souled moralists pretend, the negative quality of suffering; morality according to modern ethics is the positive virtue of energetic activity. Ours is, as the scientist correctly states, a struggle for existence; and those who consider it meritorious to succumb to injustice and violence justly go to the wall. Their enemies, unjust though they may be, are comparatively more moral, for they are their superiors in the virtue of courage which gives them strength and power.

Prof. Huxley describes how the moralist, in the effort to restore harmony, tries to account for the iniquities in this world. He says :

"From the theological side, we are told that this is a state of probation, and that the seeming injustices and immoralities of Nature will be compensated by and by. But how this compensation is to be effected, in the case of the great majority of sentient things, is not clear. I apprehend that no one is seriously prepared to maintain that the ghosts of all the myriads of generations of herbivorous animals which lived during the millions of years of the earth's duration before the appearance of man, and which have all that time been tormented and devoured by carnivores, are to be compensated by a perennial existence in clover; while the ghosts of carnivores are to go to some kennel where there is neither a pan of water nor a bone with any meat on it." * * *

This would indeed be a consistent consequence of a soft-brained and weak-hearted system of ethics, which praises the innocence and meritoriousness of mere suffering, and depicts as the ideal of morality a millennium of eternal peace, where the struggle for existence is unknown, where no labor or painstaking is necessary and all time is spent in the glorification of an all-wise Creator.

Such a state of absolute perfection is impossible and we must smile at the ingenuousness of those philosophers who pretend to teach modern ethics and still adhere to the old millennium idea of a life of perfect adaptation where universal happiness will prevail.

The error in this Utopian idea is easily seen if we understand that the struggle for existence is inherent in nature. The struggle for existence is not only not in contradiction to ethics, it is on the contrary its most important factor, which must be taken into consideration and *is* taken into consideration by the monistic view of ethics. The old ethical view demands that man shall not resist evil; that he shall leave off fighting and humbly allow himself to be trodden under foot. But the ethics of monism does not make man unfit for life, it renders him fitter in the struggle for existence. It teaches that so long as we are in harmony with the One and All of nature, so long as we remain in accord with natural laws, we shall be best able to resist evil. And this we can only do by constantly exercising our faculties and strengthening brawn and brain for the continued struggle,—which will cause us, it is true, much trouble and uneasiness, but at the same time will raise us to a higher level; it educates us and enhances the work of our existence.

The moral law is a natural law, it may be contrasted to, but does not stand in contradiction with, the other natural laws of a lower order. The deeper we investigate the more we shall be convinced that benefits acquired by injustice will prove to be injurious in the end: very often they are even the beginning of ruin. Truth and justice are the most powerful weapons in the struggle for existence. Truth and justice will always conquer in the end. It often takes more time than the life of a single individual to see the triumph of truth; but we can be sure, even if the defenders of truth and justice die, if they succumb to their immoral enemies, that truth and justice will survive.

It is the belief in truth and justice which lies at the bottom of the old religious and ethical views. This belief was a faith, but took the shape of a creed. The moral quality of a religious virtue soon ossified as a system of dogmas. It was mixed with superstitious notions, with anthropomorphic ideas, and with unwarranted phantastical expectations of a compensation in a supernatural Utopia. It grew powerful because, after all, it was more in harmony with truth than the views of those who saw only the surface of natural facts and could detect no order and no moral law in nature. But it became intolerable through the errors taught and the wrongs committed.

If, now, new ideas triumphantly break their way, let us remember that the new ethics and the religion of the future do not come 'to destroy, but to fulfil.' The present is the product of the past and the future will be the product of the present. A Latin proverb says, *Sic nos non nobis!* It is we who stand here as the representatives of humanity, but it is not for ourselves, nor for the gratification of personal vanity. It is we of the nineteenth century, but not by the wisdom of the nineteenth century, which would not exceed the wisdom of former ages if it were not benefited by their experience. Nor do we work and struggle to benefit ourselves. As our ancestors worked and struggled for us, so we have to struggle and fight for future generations.

Sic vos non vobis! Bear in mind it is you who work for the advancement and elevation of the human mind. But it is not you or you alone that you aspire for; it is humanity which is represented in you.

All life on earth forms one great, unbroken chain, one continuous whole, the unity and law of which we comprise in the formula of evolution. Let us regard ourselves as the representatives of this great whole, let us faithfully act according to this view and we need not trouble for the rest. Our actions will be moral and we shall at the same time be allied to those powers of nature which grant the strength of survival and represent advancement, progress, and the elevation of humanity. This ethics is in harmony, not at variance with natural science, and this is not the destruction but the fulfilment of the old religious faiths and their ethical aspirations.

CHRIST AND HIS ETHICS.

CHRIST and Christianity are radically different; and if the Christ of the Gospel were to come unto his own, his own would receive him not.

Christ was the Copernicus of Ethics. Naturally man believes that his ego is the centre around which the world revolves. The heathen hope by prayer and offerings or abject worship to gain the favor of God, as if they could deflect the sun and the stars from their paths in order to gratify their wishes. Christ revised the apparent order of things and taught that the ego was not the centre of existence ; we cannot make God conform to us, but we ourselves must conform to God. He forbade therefore " the vain repetitions as the heathen do," and ordained a prayer the tenor of which is characterized in the sentence ' *Thy* will be done.'

Our relation to the sun and centre of our moral life, Christ conceived under the allegory of a child to a father. Him we should imitate, and as he acts, so we should act. " Be ye therefore perfect even as your father which is in heaven is perfect."

Christ did not teach (as did at his time the Essenes and afterwards anchorites and ascetic monks) the annihilation of the ego, but he did teach resignation of all egotistic pretensions. He demanded unreserved surrender of self not for death but for life, not to destroy the souls of men into everlasting perdition but to preserve them, to comfort and heal them, to save them.

The question of worship, whether God is to be adored in the Jewish or Samaritan fashion, had become immaterial to him. God, he said, is spirit,* and those who worship him should worship him in spirit and in truth. The worship in spirit and in truth is no self-humiliating cult of adoration. Christ recognizes as his disciples not those who say, 'Yes, Lord,' but only those who do the will of his father in heaven.

It seems to be the fate of great men that their followers dwarf their ideas in proportion to the homage paid to their persons. It is certainly easier to worship Christ than to obey his commands. It is, however, our duty not to obey blindly, but to prove everything, to discard erroneous notions, and to hold fast to that which is good.

This Copernican transfer of the centre of our actions from the ego to the moral law, it seems, was the basis of Christ's doctrines. In the strength of this legitimate demand we must find the key to the success of Christianity, and we trust that it will be seen to be its surviving truth.

*The original text reads "God is spirit," $\pi\nu\epsilon\tilde{\upsilon}\mu\alpha$ $\dot{o}$ $\vartheta\epsilon\dot{o}\varsigma$, not as our translators have it, "God is *a* spirit." The introduction of the article " a " perverts the whole passage and changes a most radical conception of God into a spiritualistic view, making God a ghost.

NO CREED BUT FAITH.

By creed we understand a summary of the articles of religious belief, and by faith a trustful confidence in something or some one that we are convinced is good and true. Creed is dogmatic; faith is moral. The creeds of the world are contained in the many Credos in the doctrines of the different religions; faith is enshrined in human hearts. Creeds are dead letters; faith is the quickening spirit.

The religious problem of to-day will find its simple solution in the sentence : No creed, but faith. Let us have faith in the moral order of the world, the faith of a grain of mustard seed, and without swerving live and grow accordingly. Let us have faith in our ideals of Truth and Beauty and Goodness. If we have no faith, how can our ideals be realized? How can the tree grow if the seed be dead?

Faith in Hebrew is *amunah*, which means firmness. No credulity is wanted, but steadiness of character. Faith in Greek is πίστις, which is etymologically the same word as the Latin *fides* and the English *faith*. The verb πιστεύειν does not signify to believe, but to trust. So long and in so far as Christianity was a living faith, it was truly human and progressive. But as soon as priestcraft prevailed and identified creed with faith, the religious spirit lost its life; it became a reactionary power, for it was fossilized into the letter that killeth; and instead of faith credulity was enthroned as the basic virtue of a religious life. Not truth ascertainable and verifiable by scientific investigation was accepted as the basis of religion, but certain unverified and even absurd doctrines, which were established as self-evident axioms. Science was pooh-poohed like Cinderella as worldly and ungodly, whereas by rights it should hold the torch to faith lest it walk in the path of superstition or other errors.

Three days after the crusaders had taken Antioch (June 3, 1098), Kerbogha, the Emir of Mosul, arrived with an army which was in almost every respect, and especially in numbers, superior to the Christians. He invested the city and cut off all supplies. Famine and sickness caused great havoc, and many goodly knights, among them even prominent leaders, such as Count Stephen of Blois, deserted in great despair. The whole army seemed to be doomed to die by the sword of the Moslem or to be starved. In this plight Peter Bartholomew, a Provencal of low birth, came to Count Raymond and declared that St. Andrew had shown him the holy lance that had pierced the side of Christ, and that it lay buried in St. Peter's Church of Antioch. The search began at once; twelve men dug a whole day, and in the evening a lance was really found not far from the altar. The lance being found, the crusaders began to have confidence again. Under the command of the circumspect and brave Boemund, they went out to do battle. Although worn out by fatigue and famine, they were confident that the holy lance would lead them to victory, and full of enthusiasm they beat the Emir so that his great army was soon scattered to the winds.

The story of the holy lance, it was soon discovered by the more sober Normans, was an imposture, but among the sanguine-minded Provencals the belief in it had worked wonders of prowess and made the apparently impossible an actual fact.

There may be a living faith concealed in a foolish superstition. It is not the error, not the superstition that works wonders, but the faith that lives in it. No victory, no virtue, no strength, without at least a grain of faith, be it ever so much mixed with false notions. False notions are a disastrous ingredient in faith, and unless in time discarded, they will and must lead into danger. For weak souls, an alloy of truth and error may serve as a substitute for pure truth ; but it is truth alone that can make us strong and free.

Creed rarely can stand criticism, but faith can not only endure and survive criticism, it should even invite it. Criticism may destroy all creeds, but it will never destroy faith, and if it could, it would take out of life that which alone gives value to it. It would take away our ideals, our hopes, our aspirations, and the purpose of life. Life would be empty and meaningless.

Christ said :

"Verily I say unto you: If you have faith as a grain cf mustard seed, you shall say unto this mountain, Remove hence to yonder place and it shall remove ; and nothing shall be impossible unto you."

The instance of the crusaders' victory over Ker bogha is an example of how powerful faith can be, even though closely interwoven with superstition. It was not the superstition, however, that gave strength to the crusaders, but the moral faculty of confidence closely connected in this case with superstition. Great minds can exercise the same self-control and perform the same deeds, even greater deeds, without the

assistance of superstition. It can be said of weak
minds only, that superstition serves as a support to
faith. It is true, that if well directed, it can give to a
child the self-confident strength of a man. But woe
unto us if we mistake superstition as genuine faith.

Our faith must not be blind, but rational; it must
be based on exact knowledge, and it is our duty to
purify it by critique and to harmonize it with science.

The reconciliation of moral ideals to knowledge, of
religious faith to science is not of to-day nor of yester-
day. Ever since humanity has aspired to progress
and to increase in wisdom as well as in power, there
has been a constant readjustment of the relation of
these two factors. The prophet Hosea says :

"Hear the word of the Lord, ye children of Israel : * * *
My people are destroyed for lack of knowledge. Because thou
hast rejected knowledge, I will also reject thee."

It is lack of knowledge, or as we would now say, of
science, that threatens to be destructive. If our clergy
do not cease to preach creed, if they oppose science
because it is in conflict with their creed, they will no
longer remain priests of the Almighty, *i. e.*, of the moral
power that leads humanity onward on the path of progress. They will deteriorate into a caste of time-servers
and hypocrites, for they are lacking in the faith of the
grain of mustard seed, which is the power of growth
and progress.

Superstitions have under exceptional conditions, in
the days of man's childhood, served as substitutes for
faith; but we should learn that they are not the living
faith itself nor do they add to the strength of faith.
They rather detract from its vigor, its purity, and its
nobility. Superstitions and the lack of knowledge will
ultimately lead to perdition. On the other hand we

should learn that our faith, our confidence in the truth of moral ideals, is by no means subverted if the super-stitions incidentally connected therewith are recog-nized as illusions. Science of late has done away with many errors which had grown dear to us, but it has not and never will do away with our ideals of Truth, Beauty, and Goodness. It has rather taught us the laws according to which they can more and more be re-alized. Ideals evolve and change and, upon the whole, they progress and are improved.

If the grain rots in the earth we no longer fear that it is lost. We now know that the transformation is no sign of decay but of growth and as the husks of our superstitious notions are breaking, a new faith bursts forth which will be wider and broader, purer and greater than all the old creeds with their narrow sec-tarian convictions. Dogmas will be forgotten, but Re-ligion will remain. All the creeds will die away, but Faith will live forever.

THE IMPORTANCE OF ART.

MANY scientists and, to a great extent, business people also look upon art and poetry with a certain contempt. There are philosophers even who have no room for art in their systems or consider it as useless play—as a sport which properly should not exist, as it does not serve any real purpose.

This view of the subject is entirely erroneous and does not agree with the facts of real life. Art, and especially poetry, serve a real and good purpose in life, and are, almost as much as religious impulses, exceedingly strong. Religious sentiment induces men to sacrifice their lives for an idea, and poetical enthusiasm, in extraordinary cases, lacks very little of attaining a similar power.

Religion and patriotism have no better ally than poetry. When the Spartans waged a luckless war with the Messenians, they sent to the oracle at Delphi and requested help from their patron God, the God of light and of poetry. Apollo sent from Athens, as the legend goes, a lame school-master. But this man of seemingly little promise proved a great power,—for he was poet.

The famous verses of Tyrtæus, fragments of which are still preserved, became the leading motto of all the patriotic battle hymns in later ages, which inspired thousands and hundreds of thousands of warriors to sacrifice their lives for their country. To a great extent the sacrifices must be accounted for by a love of home and freedom. But these sentiments, no doubt, were often kindled by the glowing flame of poetry.

The influence of poetry in almost all domains of human life cannot be doubted. It is the very soul of our emotional aspirations in love, in patriotism, in religion. Poetry possesses a power directive of human passions, which may and often does lead to the elevation of human souls. Poetry is the natural vehicle for ideals. An ideal is a conception or idea of such a state of things as does not yet exist, but the realization of which is fostered in our aspiration. Poetry contains in the crystalized shape of verse certain ideas which appeal to our hearts and stir our emotions as well as our sympathies.

The harmony which obtains in versified speech makes it more impressive, so as to enter more easily into and to remain better fixed in our brains. In this way certain ideas, poetically formed and conveyed, may attain such a wonderful power as to make people stake their lives for their realization, and accordingly it is not strange that poetry was credited with potentialities and qualities that are superhuman.

Poetry in a certain sense is indeed superhuman, although it is not supernatural. The ideas often take hold of the poet, they arise in him and he seems aware of the fact that it is not he who governs them, but that they govern him.

Poetry is a formative power by which the views of whole nations are built up. 'Homer and Hesiod,' as an old verse declares, 'have given Greece her gods.' They shaped the Greek myths and ideals and exercised a decisive influence upon the literature, religion, ethics, and politics of their nation. Goethe's and Schiller's poetry told more powerfully on the formation of modern German thought than the works of all scientists and philosophers. Kant's influence on the masses is greatly due to Schiller, who confessed himself a disciple of the great thinker of Königsberg and allowed himself to be swayed by his philosophy.

If poetry is not sound, its influence is harmful. It is a fact, that after Goethe's *Werther* was published and eagerly read in Germany, suicides increased to an annual average never before reached ; and this was due to the weakening sentimentality of this one novel, which in spite of many great features is morbid to the root.

Woe to the nation whose poetry is rotten ! If poetry has grown immoral, it is the worst symptom of as peedy decay.

Germany's literature was full of promise in a time when her political prospects were extremely poor and almost hopeless. But those who saw more than the outside of things predicted her future glory. The German oak was stripped of its leaves, but the sap was sound and thriving.

There are wonderful prophesies in the German folk-lore legends, of the renewal of the German Empire and the resurrection of Frederic Barbarossa. There are prophetic poems by Rückert, Geibel, and others, which have been fulfilled beyond expectation almost literally. There is a passage in Heine's works, published in the *Salon*, originally written in French and for the French, in which the German poet tells his friends in France what the German nation will be like, if she should again be provoked to fight for her homes, her liberty, and her ideals. If she is roused, Heine said, her energy and warlike spirit will swoop down upon her enemy like a thunderstorm.

The poet is prophetic, not only because the finer nerves of his mind are quicker to understand the signs of his time, but also because his poetry is going to tell on the development of the nation. It is a strange fact, that Schiller's dramas severally forboded the events of his time. He wrote the *Räuber*, characterizing the rebellious spirit of an entire overthrow of society, and the French Revolution ensued. Then he wrote *Fiesco*, which depicted the powerful mind of a princely usurper his daring boldness and final failure, and a figure like Napoleon appeared in Europe. After *Fiesco*, he wrote *Wilhelm Tell*, the drama of national fraternity and liberty, and the *Jungfrau von Orleans*, in which he praises the marvelous delivery of a nation from a foreign yoke. Also these dramas prophetically proclaimed the suppression and the rising of the German nation, her wars in 1813–1815 and even the foundation of the Empire in 1870.

Such verses as:

> Seid einig, einig, einig!

and:

> So lasst uns sein Ein einig Volk von Brüdern
> In keiner Noth uns trennen und Gefahr.
>
> (Let us unite like brothers, as one nation
> That undivided stands in time of danger.)

exercised on incalculable influence on the German mind, which as long as this influence lasts will keep her strong and healthy and which is of greater import than her bayonets and guns.

Washington Irving has somewhere said, that it is easier to fight many battles than produce one national poem. And certainly the procreation of a healthy national literature, impregnated with great ideals and a moral spirit, is the most essential *desideratum* for the future welfare, growth, and progress of our nation. America is famous for her wealth and the American often boasts of it. Wealth is a good thing in good hands but it is a dangerous and doubtful boon in the hands of indeliberate persons, it is certain ruin and poison in the hands of libertines and slaves of passion. More important than wealth is the store of ideas, especially those ideas which are ideals, those which serve to lead us onward on the path of progress.

TRAGEDY AND THE PROBLEM OF EVIL.

ART is no mere trifling and playing, attractive and charming though its works may be. Its object is grand and serious, and its aim is not inferior to that of science.

Art and science both reveal the secrets of nature, but they adopt different methods. While science inquires into the various provinces of nature under the guidance of induction and deduction, art, intuitively grasping the idea of the whole and representing nature in single examples, gives a clew to the enigma of the world.

Every object of art is a microcosm—a little world in itself, which means, it forms an orderly arranged unity. Unity is the first and principal rule of art, which by all variety should never be neglected in any artistic production. The rule of unity teaches us that there is law and order in the microcosm of an artistic representation and at the same time suggests that the same order can be found in the macrocosm. In the creations of his imagination the artist explains the problem of the world. In his works every part must be understood through the whole, and the whole is revealed in its parts. Thus in the world and in life every single thing or being, its form, its aspect, its purport, must be interpreted as a part of the whole or as one phase in the development of All-existence. With this in mind, the Romans called a poet *vates*, seer or prophet. The poet is a priest of humanity. And, truly, of every real artist and poet one must aver, as Goethe makes Wilhelm Meister say about Shakespeare, "It is as though he revealed all the secrets of life, and yet one cannot say that this or that passage contains the solution of the riddle.'

Poetry is generally considered as the highest art, if a gradation of the arts is admissible at all. Music and Dancing, Painting and Sculpture, with other arts, exhibit a harmonious order in the rhythm of sounds or movements and in the harmony of colors or figures; they are most powerful and effective, but they do not rise to the clear conceptions of poetry, which expresses human sentiments in words and thoughts. The drama is again considered as the highest kind of poetry and among dramas the tragedy takes precedence as the profoundest, the most dignified, and most philosophic representation of human life.

Not every tragical drama is a tragedy. German æstheticians make a distinction between a *Trauerspiel* and a *Tragödie*. The tragical drama is any representation on the stage which produces mournful and inauspicious actions, while the essential feature of a tragedy must be found in the psychical development of the acting persons. The complication of the plot brings about an entire change of situation (what Aristotle calls the περιπέτεια), leading to the catastrophe. By the crisis, however, a psychical change takes place also. The acting persons, especially the hero of the drama, take another and a higher view of life and of their ideals. While the hero suffers and even dies, his ideals grow and expand. A tragical drama may represent the disastrous consequences of vice or folly only; a tragedy reveals the law of evolution which leads through toil and sacrifice to the victory of a lofty idea.

From the time of Aristotle the tragedy has been considered as the highest kind of art, perhaps because the tragic poet delves down to the deepest problem of human life: Why must the innocent suffer and why are the heroes of humanity martyrs of human ideals?

One of the greatest problems of æsthetics has been the question: How can we derive pleasure—and the noblest kind of pleasure, too—from observing, on the stage, representations of tragic events? We condemn cock fights and gladiator shows; but it is a noble pastime to witness the sufferings of a hero in a theatre. Is it not because the hero suffers for a cause, and the spectators learn from him how to live, to suffer and to struggle?

There is a law of life and of the evolution of life; and we cannot understand one phase of life without taking into consideration the law which pervades the whole. The three chief stages of psychical growth are designated by the three views of life: 1, *optimism;* 2, *pessimism;* and 3, *meliorism.*

The human being in his youth is optimistic; but when a man encounters worldly evils, when care preys upon him, sorrows worry him, and want and illness harass him, when the solemnity of death impresses his soul with fear of the unknown future, then a crisis arises in his psychical development: the catastrophe of pessimism destroys the optimistic delusions of early years, and it is but with heartrending struggles that man regains the lost balance of his aspirations in establishing a purified, a higher view of life, which we call *meliorism.*

In the phase of *optimism,* man enjoys life and accepts it as a boon which has value in itself. We live simply for the pursuit of happiness. Optimism is the ingenious conception of the child and of childlike natures. In the phase of *pessimism,* man despairs of ever being successful in his pursuit of happiness. Man learns that if happiness is the sole purpose and aim of life, life is a failure and life is not worth living. But pessimism is not the end of all worldly wisdom. *Meliorism* is taught by the martyrs of truth who suffer at the stake and the heroes of progress who die on the field of battle; they have lived a life that was well worth living. It is not life but the contents of life, our actions done, our deeds performed, and our ideas thought, that have value. Life is valuable because it is an occasion to work and to struggle, to advance and to progress. The phase of meliorism recognizes that the purpose of life lies beyond the narrow sphere of the ego; the value of life lies in our ideals, which will live after us, which, indeed, are worth living and toiling and striving for.

The philosophers of matter and motion look upon the world as a dead machine that works even in the nerves of human beings, (to use Mr. Spencer's expression), in "the line of least resistance." Monism recognizes the living spontaneity of nature which pervades the whole universe and comes to the front in God-like beauty in the moral character of man. Life, accordingly, is not a chase for pleasure but the manifestation of an effort; and Meliorism recognizes the truth "that 'the line of progress in human affairs' is very far from being the 'line of least resistance' and that in fact no great advance in some directions is possible among men without considerable work in lines of strong resistance."*

The highest art represents man as struggling for and aspiring to noble ideals, it exhibits the development from a naïve, childlike existence through the crucial tests of evil, error, and failure, through misery and terror of death to the conscious and manly standpoint of meliorism. Such a representation is the tragedy. It is not essential that the hero should die, but it is necessary that he should pass through a process of trial and purification. Thus the hero has become another man. In spirit he is new-born, and takes a new and deeper view of life and its import. The crisis of pessimism has matured his mind, and even should he die, his ideal lives; vanquished, his ideal is victorious !

In this manner the doctrine of meliorism sheds a new light on Tragedy and explains most clearly the complete sense of the Greek term, *katharsis*, or purification of the hero, which Aristotle teaches us to be the purpose of a tragedy. The katharsis should be infused into the souls of the audience through the medium of *pity and fear* (δι' ἐλέου καὶ φόβου): pity for the hero and fear in the auditor for himself lest he may meet with the same fate. The audience should be led through the same ordeal of purification. Without positive suffering, but merely by witnessing the suffering of the hero, they attain a higher, a purer, and a more ideal conception of life. It is the destruction of the egotistic passions (κάθαρσις τῶν παθημάτων), and the construction of a lofty philanthropic temple of altru-

---

*Quoted from Prof. Cope's essay: Ethical Evolution, in No. 82 of THE OPEN COURT.

ism.   The hero no longer lives for himself; he lives
for his ideals.   His ideals live in him and his life is
subservient to his ideals.   In listening to a tragedy
we are overawed; our souls are full of a sentiment
which is best expressed in the ecclesiastical term of
edification.

According to Schopenhauer and his pessimistic
adherents, the purpose of a tragedy is to preach pessimism; the hero has to turn his back upon life.   In
the school of misery he must learn to resign and deny
his will.   Schopenhauer, Hartmann,·and Mainlaender
declare that negation of will is the only aim worthy of
religion and philosophy.   It is this negation, they
declare, that tragedy has to exhibit.   But Schopenhauer did not find one instance among the ancient
tragedies in which the hero really denies his will.
Ajax commits suicide in order to atone for his errors,
yet there is nothing of negation of will.   Neither is it
to be found in Œdipus.   Hippolytus when dying is
consoled by Artemis, who promises, after his death, to
bestow upon him the highest honors in Thebes.
From these instances Schopenhauer does not conclude that his theory is wrong, as probably Lessing
would have done, to whom the ancients were the
standard of good taste; he argues that classical tragedy is shallow and inferior to the Christian dramas,
which rank higher owing to the fact of their heroes
expiring with enthusiasm.   Lessing in his *Dramatur-*
gie, mentions Christian dramas in which the heroes
sometimes rush into death with the confidence of
finding a higher and a happier existence in another
world.   We should not, however, call this a pessimistic negation of life.   They love life, but they prefer
eternity.   It is the aspiration toward some higher,

loftier state of existence which allures them to their fate.

Among our standard works of pessimistic art there is not any pessimistic tragedy, except the operas of Wagner, and particularly *Die Götterdämmerung*, in which Wodan terminates the existence of the world, and, tired of life, commits suicide. Wagner, strongly biased by Schopenhauer's philosophy, intentionally created his works in a pessimistic spirit; he is an exception. Dramas by other poets are free from pessimism, as, for instance, *Faust, Egmont, Marie Stuart, Romeo and Juliet;* the minds of the chief characters exalted by their sufferings even to death, are elevated to a higher range. They do not attain a negation of will or annihilation of the ideal to which they aspire. Just the contrary. While Romeo and Juliet die, their love lives and restores peace between the hostile· houses of their parents. In a word, our standard tragedies are melioristic and not pessimistic; for, otherwise, in their development, we should miss the solace which alone is able to afford us consolation for the misfortunes of our heroes.

The auditors profit by the experience of the hero. They grow spiritually, intellectually and morally, while he grows through his struggles. While he gains in breadth of mental grasp and in intensity of feeling, the spectators also gain. The purification of our souls, the intellectual and moral gain, in a word, the growth of our minds, is what exerts a beneficial influence and constitutes the pleasure of listening to ·a tragedy; for all growth is a pleasure: it is the only solid pleasure in life.

Schiller finds *" the cause of the pleasures we derive from tragic objects "* in " our admiration of moral propriety, which is never more vividly recognized than it is when found in conflict with personal interest and still keeps the upper hand." Schiller says: " We here (in some tragedy) see the triumph of the moral law. It is such a sublime experience that we might even hail the calamity which elicits it ; " and, further on, " How noble to violate natural interests and prudence in order to be in harmony with the higher moral law. If, then, the sacrifice of life be the way to do this, life must go." Schiller's explanation is profound and grand, but it does not exhaust the subject. The tragedy is more than a conflict between moral propriety and prudence. Such a conflict might happen in a tragedy, but need not happen. The tragedy is rather the solution of the problem of evil. The questions, What do we live for? What do we struggle and suffer for? are answered in a tragedy. We do not live for the pursuit of our happiness only, but for the struggle after, and the realization of, our ideals.

Thus the law of life and evolution is disclosed. In growing we must ultimately encounter the catastrophe and endure the hour of trial. It cannot be evaded by any one who is arriving at maturity. Our mental development starts from optimism, and, passing through the inevitable crisis of pessimism, it reaches the manliness of meliorism, which extends our life beyond the narrow limits of our Ego.

The problem as to what is the purpose of our existence is solved as soon as we recognize that man is one with humanity and that the evolution of the whole universe is at work in his aspirations. The barrier between the Ego and the All is broken and man's truest self is found in his ideals. We can find no satisfaction in the attainment of our personal well-being merely.

We must live and struggle and strive onward, not because we chose to do it, but because Nature thus works out her plans in our souls. We must, because evolution is a cosmical law. We are a part of the All, a part in which-the All works and shapes its ends. The All works in us as it works everywhere. Man is the highest stage of evolution on earth, and he therefore is the most representative part of the All we know of. Man is the first born son of Nature, and human-. ity with its holiest ideals is on earth the grandest, the most perfect, and most beautiful revelation of the All.

Man's life is a constant struggle for progress, a strife for the ideal and an advance to loftier heights on the infinite path of great possibilities. This idea is the keynote which vibrates through the highest works of art and which thrills through the universe as the law of cosmical evolution.

CLASSICAL AND ROMANTIC ART.

In art and poetry we meet with different conceptions similar to those in religion and philosophy, although they appear under other names.   There are
factions and partisans also in the domain of artistic
taste, and the most prominent oppositions are the classical and romantic schools.   These Whigs and Tories
of poetry fight with no less zeal than political parties.
The contrast is obvious and striking and you can hear
classical and romantic art spoken of everywhere.   In
music and in painting, in sculpture and in architecture
the same opposition is noticeable.

What the terms classical and romantic mean, has
been interpreted very differently and often correctly,
but its relation to philosophy has never been sufficiently
explained. Classical, it is commonly said, is that conception of art which takes the Greek of old as a standard,
but the romantic does not acknowledge either their
superiority or their taste.   Classical authors acknowledge *rule* in the domain of art, romantic authors from
a matter of principle banish rules and judge products
of art from the *effect* produced.   Classical authors on
the contrary have often shown a certain contempt for
effect and think it below their dignity to stoop to popular taste for the sake of effect.   Romanticism had always a hankering after that kind of poetry which is
to be met with so frequently in the Romance nations

that are prominently good Roman Catholics. Accordingly some literary writers of protestant Germany
identified both, declaring that Romanticism is a return
or at least the desire of returning to Catholicism. And
,it is true that many Authors of the Romantic School
in Germany turned Roman Catholics. Nevertheless
Romanticism has only a kinship to Roman Catholicism, but should not be identified with it. This may be
proved by the fact that Victor Hugo the head of the
Romantic School in France was bitterly opposed to the
Roman Church.

Among classic schools we must carefully distinguish
between pseudo-classic and real classic authors. The
Greeks must be recognized as that nation who naturally produced the classic taste for poetry as well as art
in general. Corneille, Racine, and Voltaire under the
reign of Louis XIV and Louis XV of France were the
first who attempted to establish classical taste in modern poetry. But they must be designated as pseudo-
classic; they were imitators of the Greek taste as it
had been codified by Aristotle. They did not understand the principle of classic art; they applied Aristotle's rules, but failed to recognize the spirit of Greek
poetry.

True classic poetry was produced in Germany when
Klopstock began what Goethe, Schiller, and Lessing
carried into effect with the grandest perfection ever
realized in modern literature. Beethoven's appearance at about the same time was no incidental coinci-
dence among these German aspirers. The classic
spirit of Greek antiquity was revived and resuscitated.
Theirs was no slavish imitation of the Greeks; they
like the Greeks and like Shakespeare, whom they rec
ognized as the model and standard of dramatic poetry

just as much as Sophocles, imitated nature. But they did not imitate nature in the sense of M. *Emile Zola* and the modern naturalists of France according to whom the dirt of nature is privileged with special attention. Their imitation is an imitation of nature as a whole, as one great entirety, as a Cosmos, which in its laws is one and the same throughout. Their poetry is permeated by the same unity and unison which penetrates the universe. Thus they represent in art the ethical law of justice which rules impartially, meting out to men the fates they shaped for themselves. And in the highest form of poetry in the tragedy, this justice bestows victory upon the idea which is represented in its hero. The hero dies, he sacrifices his life for what is greater than himself, for his ideal. He is conquered, the individual man with his faults and imperfections perishes, but his ideal is triumphant.

The classical principles are those of monism, while romantic art is dualistic. Classic art bears the features of serene and majestic truth, of simplicity, of reality; it is lucid and intelligible. Romantic art is artificial, complex, unreal, and fictitious; it is obscure, hazy, and mystic. Classic art has a high purpose, its aim is holy to the artist, his art is a religion to him. Romantic art attempts to fly from this world into a beyond, it is a play of fiction, a dream. Either the artist considers art as a sport, a fictitious, unreal fancy, or if he is serious, he usually is a fanatic and his poetry is not so much a religion as a superstition.

Romantic poets and artists have biased our popular views to such an extent that they succeeded to implant in the popular meaning of the word "art and poetry" the idea of romanticism, that of fictitiousness.

It is for this reason that art and poetry are characterized as a 'useless and superfluous exercise of human faculties' (as Spencer says), and that it is to be compared to sport and its value measured according to its complexity. Art and poetry are so far from being superfluous and useless that they are the most important treasures of the human race, for they contain the intellectual, the spiritual, and emotional wealth of human ideas, not of single thinkers but of whole nations, in a popular and harmonizing form so that they can easily be communicated even to the larger, broader, and less educated masses.

Goethe, Schiller, and Lessing did much to enhance and advance the idea of monism. Their poetry was the bud from which the monistic philosophy was the full grown fruit.

Classicism and Romanticism are not confined to Art. Religion also is either classical or romantic; it is either based upon clear and definite principles or upon a hazy mysticism. If Religion is not in agreement with science, it is founded upon the brittle basis of superstition. If it is in contradiction with a unitary conception of the universe, it will develop the world-despising dualism whose ideal is the oppression of nature and of all that is natural in us.

Monism in the province of philosophy means perspicuous simplicity. It is the systematic and clear conception of an intelligible reality. In opposition to the diverse dualistic conceptions of the universe in their romantic, phantastic, supernatural, or mystic garbs, monism is the classical philosophy.

RETROSPECT.

THE fundamental problems of Philosophy can . be classified under two headings:

1. What is the origin, the foundation, and the law or method of our cognition ; and,

2. What is its purpose? What is its use and application ?

The former question is theoretical, the latter practical. The former demands as an answer a conception of world and life, a theoretical philosophy, *i. e.*, a view of the universe ; the latter a system of ethics, a practical or moral philosophy, *i. e.*, a principle according to which the maxims of man's conduct can be regulated.

Our solution propounded to the former problem, is summarily named *Monism*; that to the latter, *Meliorism*. Monism and Meliorism belong to each other, the one is not complete without the other. The former is the indispensable condition of the latter. The latter is the inevitable consequence of the former.

A conception of the world and a norm of ethics will tend to find expression, not only in our thoughts as a system of philosophy, but also in our acts as morals, and even in our imagination as creations of art. Religious creeds are, to a great extent, poetical productions of the mind, expressive of some conception of the world and its corresponding norm of ethics symbolically represented as myths, holy legends, dogmas, or ceremonies.

One-sided unifications of knowledge, such as appear in materialistic as well as in spiritualistic monism (views, which in distinction from monism proper are better called henism*) will naturally lead to Optimism.

Dualism, which makes of the duality of matter and mind, of body and soul, of God and World, a matter principle, will most clearly show the dissonance of its view in its ethics. Dualistic ethics are invariably to be classed as Pessimism.

The ethical problem finds a sound satisfactory solution in Monism only, and monistic ethics are best characterized by the term Meliorism.

* Derived from " εἰς, μία ἓν *one.*"

DEFINITIONS AND EXPLANATIONS.

THE DATA of experience are perceptions.
REALITY is the sum total of all facts that are, or can become, objects of experience.
The relativity among the objects of experience we call form.
The relativity among perceptions we call formal thought.
The laws of form and of formal thought are ultimately based on the self-evident principle of *consistency*, which is the same as the logical rule of identity, $A = A$.
The order that prevails among the facts of reality is due to the laws of form.
Upon the order of the world depends its cognizability.
Methodical or systematic arrangement of experience (order among the data of experience) is possible only through the laws of formal thought.
COGNITION is the systematizing of experience.
Cognition being the systematizing of experience ultimately leads to a unitary conception of all the data of experience; it leads to Monism.

TRUTH is the conformity of cognition to reality.

[Truth being a relation between subject and object appears to be relative in its nature. Absolute truth is a self-contradiction; it would imply cognition without a cognizing subject.

At the same time it is obvious that absolute existence (in fact everything absolute) is impossible. Reality is properly called *Wirklichkeit* in German, derived from *wirken*, to take effect. Reality is not immovable and unchangeable absoluteness, but the effectiveness of things in their relations. Reality therefore implies not only existence, but the manifestation of existence also. Existence and its manifestation are not two different things; both are one.

The idea of something absolutely Unknowable is therefore also untenable; it would imply the existence of an object whose existence is not manifested *i. e*, existence without reality; *Sein ohne Wirklichkeit*—which is a contradiction, an impossibility.]

SCIENCE is the search for truth.

The method of science is the economy of thought. (*Mach.*)

Economy of thought is possible through application of the laws of form to thought.

KNOWLEDGE is the possession of certain truths.

[Knowledge is, so to say, the present stock or capital with which Science works. Science cannot exist without knowledge. The object of Science is not only to increase and enlarge knowledge but also to purify the present stock of knowledge from vagueness, errors, and misconceptions.

The purpose of knowledge is that of increasing our power over nature.]

PHILOSOPHY is a conception of the world as a system of all knowledge and of all further increase of knowledge.

[The purpose and application of philosophy is the regulation of our conduct. Different philosophies produce different systems of morality and the latter will always show the soundness or the defects of the former.]

IDEALISM is that conception of the world which takes the thinking subject as its starting point

[According to Plato the forms of things only possess reality.

Idealism, in its most advanced position, denies the existence of anything beyond subjective thought. This exaggerated Idealism is called Spiritualism.]

SPIRITUALISM explains the world solely from spirit, (*i. e.*, the substance of which the thoughts and feelings of the subject are supposed to consist) and assumes that matter does not exist. Matter is an illusion in the mind of the subject.

[Spiritualism is to be carefully distinguished from Spiritism, the latter being the belief in spirits.]

REALISM is that conception of the world which takes the object as its starting point.

MATERIALISM, or the one-sided exaggeration of the principle of Realism, explains the world solely from matter (*i. e.*, the substance of which the object is supposed to consist). Spirit is merely a function of matter.

SKEPTICISM (as taught by David Hume) is that view according to which man can have only uncertain opinions, but no exact knowledge.

AGNOSTICISM (according to Prof. Huxley) teaches that our cognition can not go beyond phenomena, and (according to Mr. H. Spencer) it assumes that cognition arrives ultimately at the unknowable.

MONISM is that philosophy which recognizes the oneness of all-existence.

According to Monism:

Idealism is right in so far as it recognizes the perceptions of the subject to be the data of experience.

Realism is right in so far as it recognizes the reality of the objects of experience.

Skepticism is justified to propose doubt as a necessary stage in the evolution of thought in order to free us from the vain assertions of dogmatism and to lead us to a critically established and irrefutable philosophy.

At the same time :

Idealism (or rather Spiritualism) is wrong in so far as it limits itself and does not go beyond the sphere of subjective perception, attempting to explain the world from spirit and the subjective element alone.

Realism (or rather Materialism) is wrong in so far as it limits itself to the material element of the object and attempts to explain the world from matter alone.

Skepticism (or rather Agnosticism, the dogmatized skepticism) is unjustifiable in so far as there are no correctly formulated problems that are not solvable.

[Science guarded by criticism can establish positive knowledge. The phenomena of nature are the facts of Reality, there is no unconditioned, no absolute existence behind them, and the idea of anything unknowable is inadmissible.]

RELIGION is man's aspiration to be in harmony with the All ; it is *das Allgefühl im Einzelnen* (the All-Feeling in the Individual.)

MORALS are man's conduct in so far as it is in unison with the All.

[The basis of morality is religion. A moral educator or preacher may justly be asked, "On what authority dost thou justify thy precepts?" And he will tell us that his authority is not personal; he speaks in the name of universal order. Accordingly his authority is that of religion. If it were not so, all his good precepts would have no foundation; they would hover in the air like beautiful dreams that have no reality.]

ETHICS is the Science of Morals; it teaches man why he must, and how he can, regulate his conduct so as to be in unison with the All.

[Religion (man's aspiration to be in unison with the All) has naturally produced many superstitious notions in the world, of its origin, and of its purpose. Similarly, science (man's search for truth) has produced many errors or false notions of reality. But all the superstitions of religion do not prove that religion as such is an illusion, and all the errors of science are no evidence that science as such is a sham.

It is obvious that religion and science, as here defined, are not contradictory to, but complementary of, each other. If religion and science do not agree, it is a certain sign that our conception of either the one or the other is wrong. The history of the human mind has been one of constant conflict and reconciliation between religion and science. Their relation has repeatedly been disturbed and re-adjusted.

The unitary conception of the world affords the only basis for the union of Religion and Science, and opens a new vista of progress for both.]

OPTIMISM takes for granted that the world and the conditions of life are good, or at least the best possible. Man lives in order to be or become happy. Happiness is the aim and end of humanity.

PESSIMISM holds that the world is bad, and that man is to be redeemed or ransomed from the evil of existence. Meditative intuition and suffering are the way of salvation. Non-existence is the ideal of pessimism.

MELIORISM stands on the doctrine of monism, that man is a part of All-existence. As a part of the whole, he has to conform to the cosmical laws of the whole. Obedience to these laws leads to a constant progress, developing ever higher forms of existence.

[The term Meliorism has been falsely used in the sense that humanity, though at present not in a state of happiness, will nevertheless reach by and by an existence in which miseries will be impossible. That, however, is a kind of Optimism. For in spite of all amelioration, happiness will remain about the same. Happiness is relative, and Schopenhauer justly likens it to a fraction, the denominator of which represents our desires and the numerator their gratifications. Every progress allows a simultaneous increase of both.

The source of error, common to both optimism as well as pessimism, is the supposition that happiness is the sole purpose of life. Pessimism is a progress in comparison to optimism; it recognizes that if the transient happiness of a life were its only end, life would not be worth its own troubles.

Meliorism reconciles the one-sided truths of optimism and pessimism. Meliorism recognizes with optimism the value of life, but not because life has an intrinsic value or because happiness is its purpose and is attainable, but because life affords an occasion of working out the possibilities of higher forms, and of realizing the better, purer, and nobler potentialities of existence. The value of life is to be measured by the efforts made in obedience to the cosmical laws.]

Optimistic morality is essentially an ennobled and elevated egotism.

Pessimistic morality, being destructive of egotism, leads to a negation of world and life. Its chief merit is that it favors the rise of altruism.

Melioristic morality considers the individual as a representative of All-existence, and thus gives a purpose to the life, to the work, and the aspirations of the individual beyond the sphere of its transient selfhood.

INDEX.

God, a moral law, 49, 151 sq.
God, a materialist, 88, 89.
God, Huxley on, 137.
God a noumenon, 144, 145, 152.
God cannot be said to be moral, 207.
Goethe on God, 152, 153.
Goethe, 76, 77, 78, 236, 241, 249.
Goethe and monism, 142.
Golgatha, 212.
Goltz, 43.
Gordian, Knot, 66.
Graphic formulas, 87.
Grassmann, Hermann, 53.
Grassmann's theory of forms, 54, 57.
Grassmann's systems' recognizes no axioms, 67, 68.
Gravitation, 89, 100, 108, 112.
Gravity, 107, 112.
Ground (grund, raison d'être), 89, 90.
Ground, qualities and reasons, 112.

Haller, 141.
Hamilton, 53, 72.
Hamilton on the unconditioned, 140.
Happiness and ethics, 218, 246.
Happiness, mere happiness, empty, 199, 217.
Happiness, relative, 258.
Harrison, 140.
Hedonism, 188.
Hegel, 59, 156.
Hegel on Space, 169.
Hegel on Time, 170.
Hegelian ontology, 119.
Hegeler, Edward C., 89,
Hegeler, Edward C., quotation on composite photograph, 38.
Heine, Heinrich, 236.
Helmholtz, 53, 66.
Henism, 253.
Heraclitus, 113.
Heresy, in mathematics, 64.
Heresy, negative criticism of, 62.
Heretics of orthodoxy, 61.
Hering, Ewald, 12, 37, 41, 42, 128.
Hesiod, 235.
Hindoo philosophy (see Veil of Maya).
Hitzig, 43.
Holbach, Baron on idealism, 183.
Holy lance, 230.

Homer, 23, 236.
Homogeneous, 122.
Hosea, 232.
Hugo, Victor, 249.
Human, factors of human existence, 17.
Human speech and morals, 220.
Humbug, the apriori, 35.
Hume, David, 32, 34.
Hume, on general causes, 89.
Huxley, on God and immortality, 137.
Huxley's agnosticism, 256.
Huxley's agnosticism, versus positivism, 173.
Huxley, quotations on ethics, 219-223.
Hydrogen, 124.
Hypermechanical, 118, 120.

Iconoclast, 154.
Idealism, 93, 94, 176, 255.
Idealism, loftier than Materialism, 94.
Idealism, Byron, and Holbach on, 183.
Idealism and realism, 176-186.
Ideals and wealth, 238.
Identity, 57.
Immanence of life, 111, 131.
Imaginary, 159.
Immanence of transcendency, 102, 104.
Immanent, 49, 91, 102.
Immanent, God, 152, 153.
Immeasurable and infinite, 170.
Immortality, Huxley on, 137.
Inconsistency, 24.
Inconsistent thinkers, 23.
Intuition, certainty of axioms based upon, 71.
Indeterminism, 191-196.
Indirect apprehension, 97.
Indivisible, reality is, 18, 93.
Inert, 113.
Inertia, 56.
Infinite, the, 159, 160, 169 sq.
Infinitude, 169 sq.
Infinity, 66.
Innate ideas, 28, 35, 70.
Intelligent and shrewd, 220.
Intelligibility of the world, 49.
Intelligibility of nature, 156.

ERRATA.

Page 75, line 17, read *certain* instead of 'ceartain.'
Page 75, line 19, read *Ansicht* instead of ' Absicht.'
Page 155, line 16, read *identity* instead of ' indentity.'
Page 205, line 15, read *they can* instead of ' it can.'
Page 236, line 16, read *a speedy* instead of 'as peedy,'

THE OPEN COURT.

PUBLISHED EVERY THURSDAY BY

THE OPEN COURT PUBLISHING COMPANY,

CHICAGO, ILL.

P. O. DRAWER F.   169—175 La Salle Street.

EDWARD C. HEGELER, Pres.—Dr. PAUL CARUS, Editor.

The reader will find in THE OPEN COURT an earnest and, as we believe, a successful effort to conciliate Religion with Science. The work is done with due reverence for the past and with full confidence in a higher future.

THE OPEN COURT unites the deliberation and prudence of conservatism with the radicalism of undaunted progress. While the merits of the old creeds are fully appreciated, their errors are not overlooked. The ultimate consequences of the most radical thought are accepted, but care is taken to avoid the faults of a one-sided view.

THE QUINTESSENCE OF RELIGION

is shown to be a truth. It is a scientific truth (a reality) which has been and will remain the basis of ethics The Quintessence of Religion contains all that is good and true, elevating and comforting, in the old religions. Superstitious notions are recognized as mere accidental features, of which Religion can be purified without harm to the properly religious spirit.

This idea is,

FEARLESSLY AND WITHOUT RESERVATION OF ANY KIND,

presented in its various scientific aspects and in its deep significance to intellectual and emotional life. If fully grasped, it will be found to satisfy the yearnings of the heart as well as the requirements of the intellect.

Facts which seem to bear unfavorably on this solution of the religious problem are not shunned, but openly faced. Criticisms have been welcome, and will always receive due attention. The severest criticism, we trust, will serve only to elucidate the truth of the main idea propounded in THE OPEN COURT.

Price, $2.00 for one year; $1.00 for six months; $0.50 for three months.
Single Copies, 10 Cts.
SAMPLE COPIES FREE ON APPLICATION.

Contents of Former Numbers of "THE OPEN COURT."

Contents of Former Numbers of "THE OPEN COURT."

THREE INTRODUCTORY LECTURES ON THE SCIENCE OF THOUGHT.

Delivered at the Royal Institution, London, during the month of March, 1887. First published in THE OPEN COURT of June, July, and August, 1887. By *F. Max Müller*. With an Appendix which contains a Correspondence on "Thought without Words," between F. Max Müller and Francis Galton, the Duke of Argyll, George J. Romanes and others. Price,. 75 Cents. The book contains three essays:

1. THE SIMPLICITY OF LANGUAGE;
2. THE IDENTITY OF LANGUAGE; and
3. THE SIMPLICITY OF THOUGHT.

Max Müller's essays must not only be read, they must be studied; and we should be very grateful that the eminent philologist uses such simple language. In spite of all the simplicity of Max Müller's style, it takes much careful study to fathom the depths of his thoughts. The study of language is of interest to the lawyer as well as the clergyman, the scientist as well as the teacher, and no education is complete without it.

THE IDEA OF GOD.

By *Paul Carus*, Ph. D. Price, 15 Cents. Contents: The Nature of Ideas—The Etymology of the Word God—God an Abstract Idea.—The Conceptions of God (Polytheism, Monotheism, Deism, Pantheism, Atheism)—Definition of the Idea of God (Entheism—Concluding remarks on Worship and Prayer).

THE PSYCHIC LIFE OF MICRO-ORGANISM.

A Study in Experimental Psychology. By *Alfred Binet*. Translated from the French by Thomas McCormack, with a preface by the author written especially for the American edition. Cloth, 75 Cents. The work contains the most important results of recent investigations into the world Micro-Organisms—a branch of comparative psychology little known, as the data of this department of natural science lie scattered for the most part in isolated reports and publications, and no attempt has hitherto been made to present them in a systematized form.

M. Binet's researches and conclusion show, "that psychological phenomena begin among the very lowest classes of beings." The author contests the theory of the distinguished English scientist, Prof. George J. Romanes, who assigns the first appearance of the various psychical and mental faculties to different stages or periods in the scale of zoölogical development. To M. Binet there is an aggregate of properties which exlusively pertain to living matter, the existence of which is seen in the lowest forms of life as well as in the highest.

www.ingramcontent.com/pod-product-compliance
Lightning Source LLC
Chambersburg PA
CBHW030348270326
41926CB00009B/1008